D0324795

UNBOUNDED LOVE

CLARK H. PINNOCK
& ROBERT C. BROW

A Good News Theology
for the 21st Century

INTERVARSITY PRESS
DOWNERS GROVE, ILLINOIS, USA

THE PATERNOSTER PRESS
CARLISLE, UK

InterVarsity Press
P.O. Box 1400, Downers Grove, IL 60515, USA
The Paternoster Press
P.O. Box 300, Carlisle, Cumbria CA3 0QS, UK

©1994 by Clark H. Pinnock and Robert C. Brow

All rights reserved. No part of this book may be reproduced in any form without written permission from InterVarsity Press, P.O. Box 1400, Downers Grove, IL 60515.

The EEC/EFTA edition published by permission from the U.S. publisher above.

No part of this publication may be reproduced, stored in a retrieval system, or transmitted, in any form or by any means, electronic, mechanical, photocopying, recording or otherwise, without the prior permission of the publisher or a license permitting restricted copying.

InterVarsity Press® is the book-publishing division of InterVarsity Christian Fellowship®, a student movement active on campus at hundreds of universities, colleges and schools of nursing in the United States of America, and a member movement of the International Fellowship of Evangelical Students. For information about local and regional activities, write Public Relations Dept., InterVarsity Christian Fellowship, 6400 Schroeder Rd., P.O. Box 7895, Madison, WI 53707-7895.

Scripture quotations, unless otherwise noted, are from the New Revised Standard Version of the Bible, copyright 1989 by the Division of Christian Education of the National Council of the Churches of Christ in the U.S.A., and are used by permission.

Cover photograph: Cowgirl Stock Photography

USA ISBN 0-8308-1853-7
UK ISBN 0-85364-634-1

Printed in the United States of America

Library of Congress Cataloging-in-Publication Data

Pinnock, Clark H., 1937-
   Unbounded love: a good news theology for the twenty-first century/
Clark H. Pinnock and Robert C. Brow.
      p.   cm.
   Includes bibliographical references.
   ISBN 0-8308-1853-7
   1. Theology, Doctrinal.   2. God—Love.   3. God—Worship and love.
4. Love—Religious aspects—Christianity.   5. Evangelicalism.
I. Brow, Robert.   II. Title.
BT78.P55   1994
230'.046—dc20   *94-26381*
                                                                                                        CIP

British Library Cataloguing in Publication Data

Pinnock, Clark H.
   Unbounded Love: Good News Theology for
   the 21st Century
   I. Title II. Brow, Robert
   230
ISBN 0-85364-634-1

15	14	13	12	11	10	9	8	7	6	5	4	3	2	1
05	04	03	02	01	00	99	98	97	96	95	94			

Introduction ———————————————————————— 7

PART ONE: Doctrine of God———————————————— 13

I   RELIGION: Models of Love ———————————— 15

II   THEISM: Creative Love———————————————— 24

III   RESURRECTION: Victorious Love ——————— 35

IV   TRINITY: Personal Love ——————————————— 45

PART TWO: Doctrine of Sin ———————————————— 55

V   DIAGNOSIS: Defective Love——————————— 57

VI   JUDGMENT: Caring Love——————————————— 67

VII   ADVENT: Active Love ————————————————— 78

VIII   HELL: Rejecting Love ————————————————— 87

PART THREE: Doctrine of Salvation ————————— 97

IX   SACRIFICE: Unconditional Love——————— 99

X   LIBERATION: Freeing Love——————————————111

XI   BAPTISM: Invitation Love——————————————121

XII   CHURCH: Window Love——————————————————130

PART FOUR: Doctrine of Faith————————————————139

XIII   PRAYER: Conversational Love ————————————141

XIV   HEALING: Transforming Love ————————————151

XV   BIBLE: Feeding Love——————————————————————160

XVI   FELLOWSHIP: Enjoying Love ——————————————168

Conclusion ———————————————————————————————177

Notes ———————————————————————————————————181

Introduction

THE GOOD NEWS ABOUT JESUS CHRIST IS THE MOST WONDERFUL PROCLAMATION
to have been issued in the history of the world. A bold claim, it announces
God's love for all people and tells us that we were all made for fellowship
with God and that though history has been spoiled by sin, God has not ceased
to love us and work toward our redemption.

The message of the Bible is the story of divine grace and human restoration. It invites us all into the joy of fellowship with God and announces his
plans to create a new humanity. But the message can be read in different
ways, and confusion about its true nature can creep in. The good news can
even be made to sound like bad news. The message can be obscured and
barriers erected which God does not intend.

Theology is the never-finished task of trying to improve upon our interpretation of the Word of God. When the vision gets blurred and the message
ceases to attract, it is time to refocus. This book is meant to help sharpen the
focus.[1]

The book developed out of an article written by Robert Brow for *Christianity Today* (February 19, 1990). Entitled "Evangelical Megashift," it called
for a revisioning of evangelical theology, especially in the all-important focus
on God. Brow is a parish priest of the Anglican Church in Canada, formerly
a missionary to India, and the author of several books.[2] Clark H. Pinnock
came into the picture as a respondent to the original article along with
Donald A. Carson, David F. Wells, Donald G. Bloesch and Robert E. Webber.
As Brow and Pinnock got together and reflected on some reactions to the
article and on deeper underlying issues, the conviction grew that there is a

shift in evangelical thinking which Brow was pointing to and which needed more spelling out. This book, then, is a fuller exposition of Brow's original vision, merged with Pinnock's parallel thoughts.[3]

What is this megashift in evangelical theology? It is an attempt to recover good news for our time. Brow was the one to call it *creative love theism*, and it is rooted in St. John's affirmation "Whoever does not love does not know God, for God *is* love" (1 Jn 4:8). It is also in agreement with St. Paul's longing that humanity be rooted and grounded in love and come to comprehend love's breadth and length and height and depth (Eph 3:17-18).

Creative love theism is a composite model with the following basic features. First, it celebrates the grace of God that abounds for all humanity. It embraces a wideness in God's mercy and rejects the idea that God excludes any persons arbitrarily from saving help. Second, it celebrates Jesus' category of father to express God's openness and relationality with us. God seeks to restore relationships with estranged people and cannot be thought of primarily as a Judge seeking a legal settlement. (The heart of Brow's original model was that we make family rather than courtroom images central.) Third, it envisions God as a mutual and interrelating Trinity, not as an all-determining and manipulative transcendent (male) ego.[4]

The model is not new—it is as old as the Scriptures—but it is a transforming truth that needs to penetrate more profoundly into minds whose thinking has been distorted by darker images. We think there may be many, inside and outside the churches, who do not perceive the gospel message as really good news for them and are, as a result, suffering. To them we dedicate this book.[5]

Creative Love Theism

The model Brow calls "creative love theism" is a vision of God who, having created us to enjoy his love, does everything to enable us to participate in grace to the full. It is a composite model designed to replace another one that has developed over centuries; this distorted model is marked by a minimizing of divine grace, an exaggeration of the legal dimension of salvation and a misrepresentation of God's sovereignty.

First, against minimizing divine grace we insist that God's love extends to all humanity (if they accept it) and not only to selected persons. Augustine taught (and the Reformers followed him) that God deliberately refrains from being gracious to an undetermined number of sinners for reasons that are completely mysterious. They call it sovereign grace, though it seems only arbitrary and stands in flat contradiction to the gospel, which declares that God desires all to be saved and come to a knowledge of the truth (1 Tim 2:4). This tradition imputes to God a character flaw by representing him as arbitrary in the distribution of grace. It would imply that those like St. Paul who weep over the lost are actually more merciful than God is in not weeping (Rom 9:1-3; 10:1). It suggests that whereas we are supposed to love our enemies, God does not always love his.

Second, over against an exaggeration of the legal dimension in salvation, we contend that seeing God as a parent is more fundamental than seeing him as a judge. Legal categories from the Latin tradition have heavily influenced theology in the West, causing the image of God as a judge to predominate in an unbiblical manner. God is both parent and judge, but it is important not to equate the two or to reverse their proper order. God primarily seeks a restored relationship with sinners, not a legal settlement. Theologians like Anselm and Calvin have led us astray when they have interpreted salvation in heavily formal and legal terms. People have gained the impression, for example, that God needed to be placated before he could bring himself to love us. But this is plainly not so: as Paul states, it was while we were yet sinners that God showed his love for us in sending Jesus (Rom 5:8). God takes the initiative in the matter of reconciliation and does not have to be placated into doing so by a third party.

Our starting point is Jesus' disclosure of God as a father who cares for us even though we are sinners. From this we take our cue that the most fundamental image is one of the family, not of the law court. Of course there is a legal dimension in the picture, because God is Judge and because the situation between God and humanity is broken in a complex of ways. But the legal aspect must not take center stage. Love and wrath do not exist in the life of God on an equal footing. We must say that God *is* love; we cannot say in the same way that he *is* wrath. We have to challenge this confusion in people's minds before it does them harm.

Third, over against a misrepresentation of divine sovereignty, we affirm the mutuality and openness of God. Another teaching that comes from Augustine, and which the Reformers repeated, sees God controlling the world so completely that there are no real surprises, nothing going contrary to his will, no disappointments. Here we confront the Hellenistic tendency to render God as an absolute principle rather than a person—contrary to the biblical portrait. In the Bible the emphasis is on God's vulnerability and openness: rather than deciding history in advance, God creates human beings with a capacity to surprise and delight him. Our heavenly Father rejoices with us when we do well and suffers with us when we are in pain. Graciously upholding our significance, God continually works to attain his loving purpose for each one of us without pushing us around. Our emphasis falls on God's generosity and vulnerability, on God's sensitivity and ability to relate to his subjects.[6]

Believers need to grow as hearers of God's Word, and we want to help. It is not good enough to repeat old slogans that may have had their day and are not very meaningful anymore. Evangelical theology does not seem to be keeping up with evangelical thinking in other areas such as biblical studies, missiology and psychology.[7] Our theology sometimes seems shallow, content not to address pressing issues. At other times, when theology does go deeper, it tends to sidestep the sorts of difficulties in traditional thinking that we want to address and correct.[8] Our hope is that this book might stir the pot and stimulate deeper explorations among us. We would like to break at least some of the complacency and stimulate more serious reflection.[9]

The book will arouse debate and cause a degree of discomfort, because it is never altogether comfortable to be asked to reconsider one's model for understanding God. In the process it can feel temporarily as if God himself were being lost, even though it is not so. That is because we tend to equate our model of God with God himself—and this we should never do. What will happen in this book is that readers will be asked to weigh competing models of God, not to decide between different gods. Critics may want to speak about a battle between different gods here, but—without minimizing the profound differences between creative love theism and the traditional model—we think this is an exaggeration.[10]

Unbounded Love is an invitation to consider God as a dynamic and loving triune being who wants to have meaningful interaction with us. Insofar as theology has allowed this vision to become clouded, we want to clarify it. There may be a great deal at stake here for some of our readers. The image of God as severe Judge and absolute Sovereign has driven and can still drive people to unbelief and despair. Modern atheism is often not so much a denial of the existence of God as the denial of a God like that one. What is needed is not arguments for God's existence but clarification of God's gracious character and actual identity.

The family model we are proposing best picks up (we think) how God relates to the world. It is Jesus' way of speaking about these matters (Paul likes to call it "reconciliation"). In the parable of the prodigal son Jesus focuses on the pardoning love of a grieving father, full of care for a wayward son (Lk 15:11-32). The boy has chosen to spurn the father's love and has turned his back, but the father still longs to welcome him home, eagerly and without reproach. The father does not think of himself in a self-centered way—he does not brood over the possessions he has lost because of his son's rebellion, and he does not worry about any affront to his honor. All he cares about is having the lad reconciled and reintroduced into the fellowship of the family. God's goal, we are meant to gather, is the joyful experience of restored relationship in his family.

This way of thinking surfaces everywhere in Jesus' life and work. It is reflected in his table fellowship with sinners, for example. Jesus said by this action that God longs to welcome people back into fellowship. In the story of the prodigal it is the elder brother who looks at things from a legal standpoint. He cannot share the father's joy because he does not think the brother is worthy of acceptance—and indeed he is not. Jesus acted generously toward sinners because he knew how God feels. God loves sinners like wayward children and longs to bring them back to communion with himself.

Reconciliation is Paul's category for salvation—a personal category, akin to a healing of relationships. God overcomes enmity and makes friends with sinners by triumphing over alienation and transforming us by grace. Paul builds on what Jesus said when he pictures God as one who takes the initiative to justify the ungodly. God's goal is that his own Son should be firstborn among many brothers and sisters in the redeemed family of God (Rom 8:29).[11]

Central to our vision is the fact that the prodigal is not merely pardoned but received back into the family with the full rights of sonship. Yes, his sins are forgiven, but what is most prominent is the father's embrace. The son is not just not-liable to punishment; the point is that he receives a warm welcome from a loving parent. It is not just that he is released from charges, but that he is restored into a loving family.[12]

What we are opposing is that development in Western theology which twists the gospel into legalistic terms, conceiving sin as primarily a disturbance of God's justice and salvation primarily as a propitiation of God's wrath. This forensic reading of the gospel portrays God not as the passionate lover of humankind but as an implacable judge. It also depicts the cross not as the revelation of a compassionate God but as an instrument of God's revenge. This is an error of interpretation that can have deadly consequences in those who accept it. We will try to correct it. We want to lift up a God who is all-loving and open to the world, and we invite all our readers to embrace the Father's heart.

The image of the creative love of God has tremendous attraction, and the gospel is itself the best apologetic. Understood properly, God is practically irresistible. It is a mystery to us why anyone would reject him who loves them so. Why would anyone reject the One whose very glory consists in everlasting love toward humans? We are moved to love God because he first loved us. The good news about Jesus is indeed a pearl of great price (Mt 13:45-46). It is the answer to any who are restless and unfulfilled, who seek for meaning and forgiveness. Life is not "a tale told by an idiot, full of sound and fury, signifying nothing" (as Macbeth said), because the universe was created and is sustained by the love of the triune God. The discovery of this reality is humankind's destiny and joy.

This book consists of four parts with four chapters each. Each part addresses a major issue. Part one considers the doctrine of God and the goal of existence as loving fellowship with the Trinity. Part two studies the hindrance that stands in the way of reaching this goal: the human refusal to receive God's love. Part three examines the provision of salvation through Jesus Christ, while part four considers the means of its appropriation.[13]

PART ONE

Doctrine
of
God

THE MOST IMPORTANT ISSUE IN RELIGION IS THE NATURE OF THE ULTIMATE or of transcendence. In any theology, the doctrine of God attempts to frame the nature of the ultimately real, which in turn inevitably affects every other concept, in particular the goal of life. At one extreme, atheism, because it posits no god, makes attainment on earth (whether individual or corporate) the final goal. A this-worldly goal has to be the final one, because in this system humanity takes the place of God and constitutes the ultimate horizon. Theism, at the other end of the spectrum, projects God as Creator of the world, with purposes for human beings, who are created in his image. In Christian theism God is a relational triune society who desires loving relationships with human persons in this life and for all eternity.

In the first two chapters we compare the various faith options in relation to this question of ultimacy. We do not make the assumption that they are saying the same things (because they are not) but want to ensure that since a choice has to be made among them, the choice be as intelligent as possible. After examining the major options, we turn in the two following chapters to an examination of Christian theism, which speaks of the goal of life in terms of bodily resurrection (chapter three) and adoption into the trinitarian family of God (chapter four). The purpose of part one, then, is to highlight the model we are calling creative love theism in terms of its doctrine of God.

I

RELIGION
Models
of
Love

CENTRAL TO THE VISION OF CREATIVE LOVE THEISM ARE LOVING RELATION-
ships, reconciliation instead of estrangement, and adoption into God's
family. The goal is to get people back into the relationship of giving and
receiving love as the Creator intended it.

In our global village it is important to discuss such issues interreligiously,
and this is how we begin. This should not be surprising—the day when we
could do theology in an enclave, without interacting with other options, is
over. In an age of increasing awareness of one another's presence in the
global setting, it will not do just to consult the issues and thinkers of Western culture and ignore the rest. Theology has been so parochial in the past, so
insular. Taking on neocolonial attitudes, we tacitly assumed that only Western religious figures and intellectuals were worth consulting. Theology done
in a ghetto cannot effectively address a world populated by people of many
faiths. Our work must be done in dialogue with other religions, and our truth
claims must be put forward in the light of what they claim. This is the way
theology must be done in the modern world, and if we Christians have
confidence in our faith, the process need not be fearful for us.[1]

Classifying world religions and their claims is not easy; their claims differ greatly on issues of the divine nature, as well as the problem of humanity and the character of salvation. It is not true that religions all say the same things, only in different culturally conditioned ways, as pluralists assume. There are important cognitive differences, and this is where we can begin.[2]

Religions can be conveniently compared overall with respect to their truth claims when we attend to the answers they give to four perennial questions that humans regularly raise:

☐ What is the nature of the ultimate?

☐ How may the human predicament be best described?

☐ What is the character of salvation?

☐ How is salvation appropriated?

What do they say about the goal of human life, the hindrances encountered in reaching it, the kind of salvation available and the means of appropriating it? The exercise of comparing religions does not favor one religion over another but allows important points to surface, helping everyone to evaluate the claims and come to a decision. Let's start with some nontheistic ideas, and in the next chapter we'll zero in on the theistic options.[3]

The first question is the goal of life. Though there are many religions, there are not as many basic answers to the question of the goal of human existence. There are a limited number of mutually exclusive ways of viewing the whole of reality and the issue of ultimacy. In our brief account we narrow them down to three basic metaphysical systems: naturalism (there is no God that matters), monism (God is everything, or the soul of everything) and theism (there is a personal God).

The second issue concerns what is wrong with humanity and what prevents life's goal from being attained. Here each religion addresses the nature of sin or evil. For the Hindu (whose goal is identity with the Absolute), evil is ignorance of this truth. For Muslims (whose goal is obedience to the law of God), sin is disobedience to divine laws. Sin is always defined in relation to the ultimate.

The third question asks what (if anything) the transcendent or the real has done about the human problem. What provision has been made? The answers range from nothing at all to everything. God can be viewed as the good that helps us simply by being there or may be seen to have chosen to send prophets or even to have come among us by assuming human nature. The Christian message puts a great deal of emphasis on what God has done in history to save humanity, but most religions emphasize what humans do to save themselves.

The fourth question considers the appropriation of salvation. This becomes an issue when the nature of the real, the problem of sin and the way of salvation have been defined. If God is Judge and sin is disobedience, obedience will be the requirement. If God is love and sin is repudiating love, penitence will be called for. If sin is ignorance, enlightenment becomes the necessary thing; if sin is inauthentic living, the means is to become authentic. Different answers are thus given to the question how people attain salvation.

Comparing Religions

With this simple procedure in hand, let us put theory into practice. Initially it seems that there are three basic types of worldview. First, there are varieties of *naturalism*—religions or quasi-religions that focus mainly on the world, whether they actually deny the existence of God or not. Second, there are varieties of *monism*—religions or religious philosophies that identify God with everything there is. Third, there are varieties of *theism*—religions that posit a personal Creator, ontologically distinct from creation, who is advancing divine purposes in history.

Here, then, are three rival conceptions about the ultimate and the goal of life between which we have to make a choice. In this chapter we reflect on naturalism, which offers salvation in the context of this world, and on monism, which incorporates a transcendent perspective on life, though usually in an impersonal way. In the next chapter we can move on to the theistic options, including creative love theism.

Varieties of Naturalism

Naturalism is the metaphysical option that takes the material world to be ultimate. It holds that there is no God of any kind, in the world or beyond it. Naturalistic spirituality operates within the all-encompassing system of nature. Because no entities exist outside the natural causal system, humans must create whatever meaning life has without bringing any God into the picture—not an easy thing to do.

Western forms of humanism look to upward evolution and the increasing well-being of humanity, and salvation comes through human effort alone. Humankind is the measure of truth and is its own only savior. One finds a natural religion of this kind in the evolutionary humanism of Julian Huxley, the existential humanism of Jean-Paul Sartre, the political humanism of Karl Marx and the egocentric humanism of Ayn Rand.[4]

Humanism is a religion even though it does not deal with transcendence. It arose as a response to a tendency in the modern era to identify God with history, with the autonomy of humanity and with the evolution of the world. Modern consciousness seemed to demand that attention be routed away from transcendence in the direction of history and the human project. There was enormous pressure to turn transcendence into immanence and to view any God as existing within the human subject.

According to deism, a second form of religious naturalism, there is a creator who does not intervene in history. Deists like Thomas Paine and Matthew Tindal imagine that God gave the world its start and its existence a basis of meaning but then left us on our own. God created the world but now lets it operate by its own natural and self-sustaining laws. Though this system does not deny the existence of God, the natural realm remains all we can be concerned about.

Deism may not be a major option today, because it is a halfway house between atheism and theism and tends either to fall into a more radical skepticism or to be drawn back into a fuller orthodoxy. After all, if God went to the trouble of creating the world, why would he not use history as a sphere of activity and revelation? Why would a good creator leave us bereft of divine assistance? Nevertheless, practical deism is widespread among many who believe there is a God but still expect to have to work out their own salvation.

There are various religions that can be placed under the heading of naturalism. Primitive religions, for example, do not deny that a high God exists above and beyond the world, but they do not expect this high God to help people. So the problems of life, such as coping with evil spirits, are this-worldly. The problem is how to attain well-being in this life, since God keeps distant and offers no real help.

This primitive outlook is more widespread than is commonly realized. Often we forget about it and give disproportionate attention to what we call the world religions. But it is estimated that 40 percent of humanity operate in the spiritual framework of a this-worldly animism. Many people who might be classified on a census as Muslims or Hindus deal mostly with magic, divination and other spirit manifestations. They are obsessed by the belief that nature is possessed by spirits that have power over human beings. Therefore one's main challenge is to gain victory over the dark powers and control power for one's own benefit through magical charms and amulets and appeasing the spirits of ancestors that roam the earth. Even though a high God may exist, he is largely irrelevant to earth dwellers, for whom the pressing need is to placate the spirits through magic, shamanism and sacrifice. Primitive peoples today are giving up the animist faith, and the danger is that secular naturalism will fill the void. In that case it is possible that their traditional life will be destroyed without anything better being given them.[5]

Religions of the Far East are mostly disinterested in a high God. Taoism, for example, honors the spirits of rivers, mountains and stars, together with the patron deities of the trades and occupations. It honors divine heroes, gods of health and good luck, and spirits of many kinds. Since the goal is oneness with nature and personal happiness, the hindrance is unnatural behavior and disharmony. The path to salvation is to live naturally. Since there is no high God to be concerned with, the individual pursues the goal of religion in relation to the material world and the natural Tao. Religion is largely a matter of adjusting to the teleology of the world and its laws.

Chinese Confucianism is similar—an ethical doctrine, a gentle humanism. Again, the goal is well-being on earth and the hindrance is anarchy in behavior. Salvation comes from living together in good relationships according to tradition. Humans become corrupt when they refuse to pursue the good of other people and of the ancestors. Of critical importance are proper relations between ruler and ruled, father and son, husband and wife. What matters is regulation and harmony, respect and courtesy, filial piety and adjustment to one's place in society.[6]

Buddhism is a world religion that in practice is largely oriented to life on earth. The Buddhist believes that our miseries arise from the desire for things. Unhappiness results from wanting this or that and being frustrated at dissatisfactions. If people could just lose their desires, they would find happiness. The state of losing desire is the goal called nirvana. It is not easy to attain, but there are disciplines available through which one can begin to lose such desire. Rather than a personal God, emptiness and the extinction of ego are central to original Buddhism. The root of misery is desire, and since there is no personal God to help us, salvation is attained through ascetic discipline, following the path laid out by the Buddha. Mahayana Buddhism tended only later to make the Buddha into a personal savior.

Zen is a Japanese variety of Buddhism whose goal is also enlightenment in this world. But the focus here is on the fact that our minds are trapped in ignorance and need to be liberated through mental discipline. Zen offers a way to experience the unitary character of reality, and since one cannot think one's way into it, what is required is a revelation that comes in a flash of insight.[7]

Varieties of naturalism, then, focus on this world. But is it really true that there is no more to existence than just this world? Love and devotion are affirmed in most religions; how can they be understood without reference to loving, personal transcendence? Living well on the earth is certainly important, and religions that foster that are making a real contribution, but there is still a deep need in us to know God. Naturalism has difficulty providing satisfactory answers to the perennial questions, Where did we come from? How did we get here? Where are we going?

Although varieties of naturalism are not models of God's love in their present forms, we are entitled to try and see God's love as it seeks to penetrate them. With St. Paul, we hope that all such people will feel after God and find him, since he is not far from any one of us (Acts 17:27).

Varieties of Monism

The second major metaphysical option is monism, which identifies God with the world or with the soul of this world. God is not thought of as distinct from the world, and transcendence is equated with the material world. The truth claim here is that reality is ultimately one. God is the world, the world emanates from God, God is in the world, and through the world God himself experiences change and evolution. The world in both its good and its evil flows from God *necessarily* and is not the result of any decision on God's part. Since monism is hard to reason one's way through, its truth is grasped mystically rather than by rational inferences.[8]

Monism too appears in different forms and subtle variations. The absolute pantheism of Parmenides recognizes only one being; the emanational pantheism of Plotinus sees everything flowing from God; the developmental pantheism of Hegel sees God unfolding historically in time. In one way or another, the finite things (including human beings) are forms of an absolute substance that is not personal. Unlike naturalism, monism is God-centered, for it posits God as the essence of all being. Monism can be viewed metaphysically as intermediate between theism and naturalism.

In Western culture, *panentheism* is becoming more popular. Related to pantheism, this system preserves a greater degree of transcendence. Rather than completely identifying God and the world, it views God as being in the world as the soul is in the body. Panentheism is really an attempt to move monism closer to theism. It preserves a degree of divine independence from the world but still sees God as enmeshed in the process of worldly change, not in a voluntary way but in a relationship of necessity. Panentheism is monism modified in the direction of theism in avoiding any simple identification of God and the world. Theists should encourage panentheists to take things further in this direction and admit that God is the creator of the world and involved in it voluntarily. Without that there is no God who is really ultimate.

Philosophical Hinduism embodies monism in a classic religious form. In the thinking of Shankara (d. 820), salvation has an eternal dimension, though not on a personal plane. The goal of religion is oneness with being, and humankind's problem is that we do not recognize or acknowledge this. This makes knowledge the key to salvation: we must learn to recognize our own divine identity. We need to change our way of thinking and accept the fact that we are part of the divine essence.

An influential form of Hinduism in the West has been that of Radhakrishnan (d. 1975), who posited different levels of reality and considered the Absolute to be manifested on all the levels. Our main need, he thought, is always to negate the ego, tune into the divine ground of our being and hope to overcome the cycle of rebirths. The individual is an aspect of transcendence and aims at union with God.

In monism God is impersonal and the world is a projection of the divine essence. What we call the New Age markets this monistic thinking in the West. New Agers like to say that all being is one, interrelated and interdependent, and that God and the world are all part of one continuous reality without boundaries. Everything, including ourselves, partakes of this one divine essence. Whatever exists is god and is therefore perfect. Humans are divine and only need to wake up to that fact, to honor and worship themselves. People need to realize the full potential of their divinity, overcome the ignorance of this truth of their being and alter their consciousness so as to become aware of basic oneness. New Age spirituality promises to help us tap into spiritual energy within ourselves. It is a Western form of monism that places emphasis on the individual, although (paradoxically) the idea of monism originally was to lose personal distinctness.

Monism gives rise to questions in the mind of a thoughtful listener. How can we be one with Being when we sense our own personal distinctness as a fact—our being distinct from other persons and from God, and our being persons who crave fellowship with God and other people as other than ourselves? If God is impersonal, there can be no genuinely I-Thou relationship with God, though the need for such a relationship is fundamental to religions, including popular Hinduism. This must be why monistic religion tends to develop theistic cults such as Hare Krishna. Monism also has special difficulty handling the problem of evil because it is forced either to declare it illusory or to attribute it to God—and neither option is very satisfying. And it gives no real significance to human beings but makes black flies as important as we are. The goal is to escape individual personality, even though being persons is surely what we most essentially are and want to be.

In its usual forms, monism is not a model of love. It does not aim to introduce people to fellowship with a loving God. But monists do celebrate the mystical fact of our living in God and may therefore be drawn by the Spirit to refine their understanding of who exactly it is in whom "we live and move and have our being" (Paul here quotes from a monistic poet in Acts 17:28).

Understanding and Choosing
We need to be fair as we compare the basic religious options. We care about what other people believe. In natural science one can classify the mammals, for example, without having to decide whether lions are better than whales or rabbits preferable to donkeys. Such decisions are required of us in other contexts, such as when we have to settle between adopting a cat or a skunk as a pet. But there is a place for making an effort to understand the inner logic of each way of viewing life without necessarily choosing to pursue any of them. On the other hand, individuals may wish to convert or be converted. They may want to switch from one way of looking at things to another way, from one model of faith to another one.

In this chapter we have confined ourselves to classifying religions without making many value judgments. Eventually, of course, one has to make a choice whether to be a Marxist or a Jew, a Quaker or the devotee of a guru. After making comparisons, one might decide that one religion or ideology is not as appealing as another as a way for ordering life. Buddhism, for example, would be unattractive for a person who wants love and to be loved to the full. Or choosing to flow with the law of the Tao would be unappealing to someone who is seeking to be saved from hell.

We are not left with relativism in religion by pursuing this route. In the process of comparison we find that there is room for persuasive argument. Often it is practical argument based on the implications of being committed to one kind of goal or another. God has given us freedom to choose how we wish to order our life, and the choice is not to be made only by logic. Our analysis has confined logic to the inner structure of each system; no one can be forced by superior intellect at the point of decision. Obviously God knew that if people could be converted by logic, only the intelligent person could be saved.

Accounts of Love

Religions can be viewed as alternative accounts of love. Consider these statements, which use the word *love* in ways that have very different implications for life.

☐ If you love God enough, he will love you, but if you do not, you will be sent away.

☐ Love is a desire that requires eradication if one is to find genuine peace.

☐ Love requires respect for ancestors and submission to leaders and to established structures of society.

☐ Love is attained by gaining the freedom to do as you please regardless of the feelings of others.

These statements about love can be and have been developed into religious systems that enshrine quite different pictures of what love is about and thus how one should order one's life.

What we want to argue in the next chapters is that the way of ordering one's life called creative love theism is the best way to make sense of life. It places one in relationship with a loving, personal God who desires the love of all made in his image. As we proceed, we should remind ourselves that the love of God was not invented by Christians in the New Testament. God's love was already at the heart of the Old Testament. There are about eighty references to the steadfast love of God (RSV and NRSV) in Psalms 5—130, and Psalm 136 mentions that love in every one of its twenty-six verses (see Gen 32:10; 39:21; Ex 34:6-7).

II
THEISM
Creative
Love

Iɴ ᴛʜᴇ ʟᴀsᴛ ᴄʜᴀᴘᴛᴇʀ ᴡᴇ ʙᴇɢᴀɴ ᴛᴏ ᴀᴘᴘʟʏ ᴀ ᴍᴇᴛʜᴏᴅ ꜰᴏʀ ᴄʟᴀssɪꜰʏɪɴɢ ᴛʜᴇ religious models people use to order their lives, starting with nontheistic (naturalistic and monistic) options. Though much is admirable and true in them, the survey leaves one wondering whether there is not more to religion. Isn't there another quite different option? Particularly disturbing is the absence of a personal relationship with God, which undercuts prayer and loving interaction. This lack denies the hunger of the human heart for such interaction. One major strength of theistic options is that they offer the possibility of I-Thou relationships.

Varieties of Theism
Theism is a metaphysical system that posits a personal God existing beyond and within the world. God is a personal agent, the world is a creation, and history is a sphere for the outworking of divine purposes. Theism sees God as an infinite-personal being, the maker of heaven and earth, who values human beings made in his image. In the Christian version, God cares about humankind so much that he enters into history to restore the covenant relationship threatened by sin.

Theists see God as the Artist-Creator of the world. In the biblical account of creation, God declares the work of his hands very good. Who would not join in the refrain and marvel at the grace that called the world into existence in an act of sovereign freedom? God was in no way compelled to make the world, but by grace he gave existence to other beings and entered into a relationship with them which, in spite of their finiteness, he views as worthwhile and delightful. Because God creates with purpose, the world is a dynamic and purposeful place. God did not create it and then withdraw and stop working. His creation was the beginning of a history open to the future and ever moving toward the goal God set for it.[1]

Contrary to the claims of some, belief in creation does not entail denying evolution except in a secularist form. Developments have taken place over long periods of time in the history of the world. What the sequence of events was and exactly how long the process took are questions for scientists to explore, not for theology to decide. God could have created everything suddenly if he chose to, but he is not bound to work fast. A day of God's is as a thousand years on our calendar. Evolution as such does not require a naturalistic worldview—God has lots of time to play with.[2]

We ought to think of creation not as a scientific theory about origins but as an affirmation of our faith in the Creator. Theology and science tend to speak different languages that can be related in complementary ways. It is not wise to provoke a warfare between them. Faith in God the Creator and an assumption that God worked through some form of gradual development of the natural processes can be held together.[3]

Deism also posits a transcendent Creator, but unlike theism it denies that God acts purposefully in history subsequent to creation. It maintains that the world operates according to naturally self-sustaining laws and views God as a kind of watchmaker who, having wound up the clock, leaves it to operate on its own without intervening further. The God of deism has no particular purpose for humans in the world, who have to figure out what is right and wrong by studying nature and who live their lives without a personal relationship with their Maker. On the last day all will stand before him and be judged according to their performance. This feature makes deism similar in practice to forensic theism (discussed below), except that it depends on a natural rather than a supernatural revelation of God's law.

For theism, the Creator-Artist has a purpose for everything that he has made. It is a powerful vision that gives solid meaning and significance to our lives. This may explain why nontheistic religions develop theistic cults. The idea that there is a personal God, creator of the world, who has a goal for history and purposes for humanity, has tremendous appeal. It offers an explanation of how the world came into existence, why it is so delicately ordered and for what reason it was made. This appeal moves people in the direction of theism as soon as the idea of God's desire for fellowship with humans is recognized.

The Forensic Model of Theism

All theistic models make a personal relationship with God possible, but not all agree on the basis and nature of that relationship. Islam, for example, is a major theistic world religion that has become Christianity's main competitor. It lifts up the majestic transcendence of God and emphasizes his character as awesome Judge. Muslims confess Allah as the one true God and Muhammad as his apostle, seal of the prophets. Islam claims that God gave a revelation of his will for humanity through the Prophet which was recorded in the sacred Qur'an.[4]

Islam's doctrine of sin is understood in relation to these features: it is a failure to submit to God's will as expressed in Qur'anic law. Islam has developed five pillars: the simple creed confessing Allah and Muhammad as his Prophet, regular daily prayers, fasting, almsgiving and pilgrimages to holy places. Humanity's prospect is a final judgment in which their lives will be evaluated on the basis of their having followed and observed God's will. Deeds will be weighed, and people will receive what they deserve. There is no savior or atonement; each person is solely responsible for his or her fate. One's fate is fixed as one adheres or fails to adhere to the commandments. Islam is an uncompromisingly *forensic* (law-based) model.[5]

Islamic theism, then, is contractual. There is a forensic arrangement in which God demands obedience and gives salvation on the basis of one's efforts. Whether such a religion is a burden or not depends on what God has commanded. Fortunately for Muslims (and this gives Islam considerable appeal), what is commanded is not too stringent but fairly easy to fulfil. Sin is not taken to involve inner corruption, and it is assumed that people are able to obey God's will in their own strength. Having done what is required, the faithful are entitled to feel good about their achievements.

Law is also a central category in the Bible. But the religion of Israel was not originally a religion of works-righteousness, even though at the time of

Jesus and today among the Jews it may be so interpreted. The category of law can be taken either covenantally or in a moralistic direction. In our view neither Judaism nor Christianity was intended to be a religion in which acceptance with God was earned through works-righteousness, though both were taken in that direction by some adherents.[6]

In some forms of Christian theism, legal categories tend to predominate. A broad Western tradition from Tertullian, Augustine, Anselm and Calvin has had a markedly forensic character, viewing God as Judge and salvation as in some way a contract. Brow's original protest concerned this mistaken interpretation. He objected to the tendency to change God from the lover of humankind to an implacable judge.

The Westminster Confession, for example, speaks of a covenant of works that God established with Adam in the beginning, a contract that promised life on the condition of perfect obedience. Such language is of course contractual, and the law court is central to the thinking of such a "federal" theology (the Latin *foedus* means covenant). In this model, sin is viewed as an infraction of God's rules, atonement is needed to appease his wrath, and salvation is conditioned upon Christ's being received. The legal category of justification becomes key and is divorced from the context of personal relationships. The system implies that God loves people only when the penalty has been paid in full and all the conditions met.[7]

Forensic theism may be predestinarian as well, as it is in the Westminster Confession. It turns out that those who receive the imputed righteousness of Christ are enabled (compelled) to do so by the irresistible power of the Spirit. This point was added by Augustine to preserve (as he thought) the gratuity of grace and the sovereignty of God in salvation. In this way God alone can be said to decide who will be saved, and there can be no appeal since there is no basis on which sinners could object. God's saving operations are directed only toward those individuals chosen to be saved; the others are passed over.

Tensions arise because legal categories conflict with deterministic ones. Law speaks of conditions that have to be met, while predestination declares that they cannot be met. In order to be saved, one must meet the conditions of the covenant, but one is unable to do so without divine coercion. In neither case does history have real significance.

But there are forms of theism that maintain God's gracious and interactive character and see him as a loving person. In creative love theism, humans are not puppets manipulated by God but agents created to hear and respond to God's Word. The purpose of their existence is to enjoy fellowship with God, and sin is understood as a turning away from God's love, while salvation is a new relationship in the family of God.

Catholic and Evangelical Models

Creative love theism is now a common idea if not an organized model among many Catholics as well as evangelicals, but it was not always so. The Tridentine version of Catholicism (before the Second Vatican Council) viewed the institutional church as the earthly context of the believer's relationship with God. Emphasis was placed on the benefit derived from rituals performed by the holy priesthood. In this system, salvation comes from God and not from human effort, but grace is channeled nearly exclusively through priestly ministrations. What God accomplished in Christ for salvation is available to men and women through the mediation of the church, understood as a supernatural institution representing Christ and perpetuating his redemption. Through the church Christ continues to function as prophet, priest and king. God provides salvation but has placed access to it under the control of a system of earthly mediation. The church thus became the mediating agency, the proximate source of grace through its ordinances.[8]

The danger in such an orientation is that people are tempted to trust in the church rather than depending on God alone. Grace is given the appearance of being on tap in the institution and at the disposal of the clergy. These operations, being at the disposal of humans, may be easily diverted to serve the controllers' own ends.

With the reforms of Second Vatican Council, however, it has become more common in the Catholic Church to focus on God's working through the earthly *signs* of church and sacraments, touching and transforming our lives. Many Catholics and Protestants now see the church as the sign of God's redemption and their spiritual mother, not so much as an institution dispensing salvation.

Creative love theism may assume such an ecclesial and sacramental mode. It sees God working through ordinary people, through physical and material realities, to communicate healing in people's lives. As in the incarnation, God uses the created order as a vehicle of his saving and healing presence. Because human nature is social and communal, in the church we can encounter the mystery of God.

Creative love theism also assumes a more evangelical form which puts relatively less emphasis on the church and relatively more on the faith of believers. At the same time, loving relationships remain central. The evangelical version maintains a high doctrine of the church, but it treasures the biblical metaphors of parents and children, brothers and sisters, friendship and reconciliation, adoption and homecoming, the family table and Eucharist.

Judge and Father

Creative love theism celebrates a different set of theological categories from those of the forensic model. Even when the images overlap (both models see God as Judge, for example), the meaning is somewhat different. When it thinks of God as Judge, creative love theism does not think of him as a law-court judge, but as a judge of the biblical type (recall how judges in the Old Testament cared about liberating oppressed people and putting things right). Both models may speak of God as a king, but with different views of the meaning of sovereignty. When creative love theists think of monarchy, we do not picture an all-determining power but a Davidic king who protects and shepherds his flock and delegates power to others. Jesus' metaphor of the Father who loves us unconditionally is the central image in creative love theism rather than Judge or Sovereign, and it controls the meaning of these other metaphors.

In forensic theism the biblical metaphors are used rather differently. Seen as a courtroom type of judge, God can display parental love only after the penalty has been fully paid. His wrath would have to be satisfied before any love can flow. In this model, original sin is understood as the imputed guilt of another, whereas in creative love theism it is seen more in terms of estrangement from God and as an oppression that impacts us from birth and from which we need liberation.

In forensic theism, "vicarious substitution" refers to Jesus Christ's legal acceptance of the penalty due to us and the transfer of his righteousness to our account. But in creative love theism substitution has a much broader meaning. In the entire life, death and resurrection of Christ there is a vicarious element whereby the Incarnate One takes humanity through death into resurrection. Substitution is inherent in all the forms of loving, whether in risking one's life for a friend or in all the chores parents do for their children.

For creative love theism, sacrifice is not so much a legal metaphor of payment for sin as a handing over of one's life to God in loving surrender. The crucifixion is viewed by forensic theism as payment, the settling of a penalty, while in creative love theism it becomes the historical expression of the suffering heart of God. At the cross the three persons of the Trinity experience the hurt of loving sinners and, by this act of sacrifice, open up a path to reconciliation.

The Trinity, Creation and Sin

The forensic model creates difficulties for trinitarian theism because it pits one person against another. The Father as judge is compelled to condemn sinners to hell, whereas the Son as savior pleads for humanity and pays off their penalty. When the offer is accepted, God is free to love us and the Spirit is free to begin his work in us—but not until then. In creative love theism, on the other hand, all three persons of God share in reconciling and drawing us into loving conversation. All three love us unconditionally, all three are present with everyone, all three share the work of bringing us to glory before we ever respond.

Trinitarian theism is a unique kind of theism. The one God is at the same time a family of loving relationships, a fellowship of giving and receiving, a dynamic sphere of personal interaction. And the triune God created a world where loving interactions could occur on the human level, thus echoing love back to himself. The creation can then be seen as the freely given gift of God's grace and love. This leads us to define sin as the decision of the creature not to welcome love (divine or human), not to want to give and receive, not to welcome the loving reciprocity that is basic to God's nature and to our own. God's response to this refusal, however, is not to give up on humanity but to keep on giving graciously in even deeper ways. In the face of betrayal, God's decision is to give his own Son as a sacrifice of praise on behalf of us all and to send the Spirit to lure us back to the fellowship of giving and receiving for which we were created. The goal of salvation is to experience the kind of sharing love that is basic to God's very nature.

What Heaven Is Like

Each type of theism gives life in the new creation a different flavor. Forensic versions view heaven as a reward for obedience. In Islam it is reward for obedience to the laws of Allah. In ritualism it is reward for obedience to a set of rituals. Heaven is a place where the obedient are justly rewarded, a place where they can enjoy pleasures denied on earth. Fellowship in a family is not its nature.

In creative love theism, heaven makes possible a flowering of the love relationship begun on earth. The glorification of God's children from all races and all times is pictured as a city, the new Jerusalem, where all are loved and free to love. The letter to the Hebrews says that Abraham looked forward to this city, whose architect and builder is God (Heb 11:8-10). Abraham and Moses are called God's friends, and Jesus called the disciples his friends. From this we deduce that the friendship with God begun on earth flourishes with God and with others in the eternal city.

The goal of life is to enjoy open friendship with God and with one another. When we speak of God's creativity, we refer not merely to the beauty and variety of plant and animal life but to the fact that God made us to love and to enjoy loving to the full. Not a reward for obedience, not an outcome of a sacramental process, salvation is reconciliation and the restoration of these relationships.

Creative love theism affirms that all of us were created by the divine Artist for the joy of perfect love. God is love, and we who are made in God's image are made for love, for God's perfect love. The Artist-Creator is our loving Father, who wants his children from all the nations to come home to his family.

The Loving Parent

God's fatherhood is the root metaphor of creative love theism. The metaphor was already in use in the Old Testament. The intent was not to identify God as a male, since God is beyond gender. This is confirmed by the fact that God is also pictured in female images: as mother who protects her children like a hen, nurtures them from her breast and never forgets how much she loves them. Isaiah pictures God as a pregnant woman crying out in labor (42:14). God, who is not a sexual being, needs both human genders to represent himself. The point of such gender-specific metaphors is that God is like a loving parent, continually working to provide an environment designed to free people for the joy of loving.

We should not draw the wrong conclusion from the fact that Jesus called God his father, as if he meant that no other language could be used for God. Jesus felt free to speak of God as a woman searching for a lost coin, as a

shepherd looking for lost sheep and as a woman kneading her dough. There
is a fluidity of language here. Besides, Jesus' idea of father was not of a
patriarchal figure who is fond of domination but of One who upends power
and calls for mutual relationships.

The model of creative love theism celebrates three divine persons in the
oneness of God. The Father is the loving source of our being. The Son beams
forth the light of God and comes alongside us to befriend us. The Spirit
works from within to inspire, guide and free us to love. Because God is love,
we can be sure that no one will be excluded from knowing God by ignorance
or lack of opportunity. Only those who deliberately reject God's love will be
excluded, and they will really have excluded themselves. God has decided to
exclude no one—exclusion can happen only as a result of the human
decision to love darkness rather than light (Jn 3:19-21).

Faith is what pleases God (Heb 11:6). Once one begins to relate to God
as friend, one's heart is oriented in the direction of salvation. While truth is
involved, no one knows how much knowledge is needed for a person to have
faith. Believers such as Job and Abraham in the Old Testament had limited
understanding but were justified by faith just as we are. God accepts or rejects
persons by faith—not on the basis of how much knowledge they possess but
according to the direction in which they are heading, whether toward or
away from God. One can receive a gift without knowing exactly who it comes
from. In the same way sinners can receive God's love with limited understanding. Faith may even occur in the context of another religion, since the
issue is not how far one is from God but in what direction one is now
traveling.[9]

Revelation

Theists have a strong view of revelation, because if there is a personal Creator
who loves us and wants us to know him, he would have to communicate with
us so that we might know his thoughts and plans. God would have to make
himself known. Though we sense God's presence in many places, Christians
see God's revelation especially in the history of Israel and in the life of Jesus,
where God has taken the initiative and freely communicated with humanity.
Not content just to give information, God has shared his very self with us in
the narrative of the gospel set forth in the Scriptures.

Revelation, then, does not refer to the Bible in the first instance but to
God's revelation in history. Yet we would not know much about that revela-

tion were it not for the biblical witnesses. Through this testimony, human though it is, the Spirit brings about a true knowledge of God. This does not mean we should take the words of the Bible naively, at literal face value without any effort at interpretation. God's revelation comes to us mediated in human forms; it does not give us direct access to God's essence. What we know about God surfaces by way of the stories and metaphors the Bible gives us. Our models are constructed as we organize and interrelate the metaphors. This is a human and an imperfect activity. Problems arise when people assume that their construal of the metaphors is the only possible one and catches the very essence.

As evangelicals we are committed to a high view of the Bible as attesting God's revelation, and we believe that the model of creative love theism fits God's revelation comfortably. But ours is only one model among others, and we respect the right of other people to construct their own model for organizing the metaphors. We reject the pretensions of those who insist that their model for interpreting the Bible is the only one that is valid.

Testing Religious Claims

Atheists believe that all religions are false, but Christians do not have to say this. We take a more liberal view of such things. We are free to think, for example, that most religions contain some truth or hint of truth. We believe that the Spirit of God still moves over the face of the deep. We are not required to believe that most of the race has been wrong when it comes to the matters that concern them most. Religions are human efforts to find the truth, and we must consider what they claim to have discovered. God is reaching out to all humanity, and we see religions reaching out to God, each in its own way. There are many profound perceptions of God and truth codified in world faiths, and we respect and take them seriously—as seriously as we take varying insights in philosophy and mathematics. God is revealed everywhere in his creation, and there is revelation also in the history of religions. But since the religions do not all say the same things, decisions have to be made. Truth claims have to be weighed and evaluated.[10]

But how does one evaluate and assess the truth of religion? Is it just a matter of taste and opinion, or are there more objective criteria? So far we have stressed the pragmatic basis of faith. As we have sorted through religious options, we have mused on which are most attractive to us. This is natural for Christians, because the gospel has immense attraction as a "pearl of great price" that offers meaning and hope, forgiveness and fellowship with God.

According to Jesus, the God who made the universe loves us and wants to relate to us. What could possibly give us a greater sense of importance and value than that? At the depths of the Christian revelation is the truth that human history is being redeemed by the grace of God at work. We long for every person to gain knowledge of the ocean of God's love.

The Christian message is really good news, and what strikes us about the other options is the relative lack of good news. Not that other faiths have nothing of value to offer. It is good, for example, that practitioners of religions that are oriented to this world pursue righteousness and peace. It is good that practitioners of religions seeking union with God should do so diligently. But beyond these things, what humanity needs is a loving God as the source of our life.

The good news came into being because of Jesus, who announced the love of a God who wills the wholeness and humanity of everyone, especially the poor and heavy-laden. Jesus came into the world to gather outcasts under the wings of God. In his parables and through his mighty works, he proved the reality of God's goodness and unleashed hope and healing. His love for us was so great that he tasted death on our behalf, but the Spirit restored him to life and formed a people to make the good news available to everyone on earth. We call upon those of every faith to come higher up and go deeper into God.

The pragmatic test is a good place to begin in the validation of religious truth claims, but of course it cannot be the only consideration. There are truth questions to be considered; our pursuit cannot be reduced to a competition to see who might offer the most existential benefits. There are questions of credibility and coherence, issues of adequacy and experience, issues of rationality and history. Everyone must look at the pattern of the evidence and decide for themselves.

We are all on a pilgrimage through life, and we live in advance of the time when truth questions are fully resolved—as they will be at the end of history. In the meantime there is no choice for us but to walk by faith, not by sight. We may feel lost in the woods, but if our heart is open to God, the truth will dawn on us.[11]

III

RESURRECTION
Victorious
Love

ACCORDING TO THE BIBLE, THE GOAL OF HUMANITY IS BODILY RESURRECTION in the context of a renewed creation. The raising of Jesus of Nazareth proclaims hope for all humankind and for the whole creation. As St. Paul declares, "As all die in Adam, so all will be made alive in Christ" (1 Cor 15:22). Resurrection is the cornerstone of Christian faith—it proves that Jesus is Lord and that God's kingdom will come as promised.[1]

At the end of the last chapter we spoke about pragmatic grounds of faith; now we can say something about the historical basis. Because of prior beliefs, an atheist might not be convinced, but there are strong reasons for believing that God raised Christ from the dead. A surprisingly good case can be made for it.

The facts are fairly simple and straightforward. The event was a surprise to Jesus' disciples, who forsook him and fled after his arrest. The tomb in which the crucified Jesus had been laid was found to be empty, and his followers began to experience encounters with the risen Lord. From that point a movement started based on belief in Jesus' resurrection—a movement that continues to this day.

All this is well documented in the New Testament, and there is no hint of deception in it. The dejected disciples were transformed by this event and by the outpouring of the Spirit on the day of Pentecost. The rest is history. Some people will not believe this, however much evidence is adduced. They will concoct some reason or other why the tomb was found empty. But others who are more open to God breaking into their lives may find the case as persuasive as we have.[2]

The meaning of the resurrection is linked to the hope of new creation. As the cross speaks to the sinful past, so the resurrection speaks to the redeemed future. It is not just an isolated event that happened to Jesus—it is the firstfruits of the resurrection of the dead at the end of time. It signals the birth of a new order and opens the future for all of us. Jesus brought immortality to light and anticipated in his resurrection a world transformation. His resurrection tells us that there is fulfillment beyond this life and that death will not have the final word. The Risen Lord is the embodiment in advance of a new creation in which we can all share.

The promise of resurrection is one of human life fulfilled and perfected in the presence of the triune God. Instead of a merely worldly salvation, monistic oneness or judicial acquittal, the gospel of resurrection speaks of new creation and a personal and social fulfillment for which we were created as covenant partners of God.

Resurrection is a leading motif of the New Testament proclamation. As Peter states, "God . . . raised [Jesus] from the dead and gave him glory" (1 Pet 1:21). Paul could call his message "the word of life" because resurrection was central to it. Because of it believers can experience the power of his resurrection now and new life in the age to come. The resurrection has a clear meaning for us personally. It takes away our fear of death. It means that we can walk through the valley of the shadow and not fear evil. It means that our relationship with God is stronger than death. Paul puts it this way: "[God] will transform the body of our humiliation that it may be conformed to the body of his glory, by the power that also enables him to make all things subject to himself" (Phil 3:21).

The resurrection was the focus of apostolic preaching in the book of Acts. It had to be, because without it our faith would be devoid of basis and meaning. Paul says, "If Christ has not been raised, then our proclamation has been in vain and your faith has been in vain" (1 Cor 15:14). This is so because salvation comes through faith in the crucified and risen Lord. "If you confess with your lips that Jesus is Lord and believe in your heart that

God raised him from the dead, you will be saved" (Rom 10:9). The resurrection is the foundation and central message of Christianity.

The Cross *and* the Empty Tomb

Though resurrection is central in the New Testament, it has not always been central in theology. The same Latin traditions we have referred to, according to which Christ is said to appease divine wrath on the cross, leave no room for resurrection to be central. Because the theory considers the work of Christ to have been finished on the cross, it diminishes the importance of the resurrection. It prevents the Easter event from playing a central role in redemption.

We need to get used to thinking that people are saved not by the cross only, but by the cross and resurrection of Jesus. Paul says this plainly: "If while we were enemies, we were reconciled to God through the death of his Son, much more surely, having been reconciled, will we be saved by his life" (Rom 5:10). Why would Paul say that? Who ever heard a theologian say that the resurrection was more important than the cross for salvation?

Indeed, why was the resurrection of Jesus so important for the early Christians? Obviously, for the first disciples Jesus' resurrection would have been an unexpected happy surprise. It would have encouraged them mightily to know that the crucified Lord was alive. But there must be more to it than that.

Perhaps some people make the cross more central than they should because they think they understand its rationale tolerably well, whereas no such rationale springs to their mind about the resurrection. The history of Christian doctrine offers little discussion of theories of resurrection comparable to the vast discussion of theories of atonement.

Theology of Resurrection

Another problem is that we moderns tend to think of Jesus in a very individualistic way. We need to train ourselves to see him more biblically, because Jesus saw himself (and the New Testament writers saw him) as the last Adam and as a representative of humanity. Not just an isolated individual, Jesus was also a corporate person who intended to identify with humankind in his incarnation, life, death and resurrection. "Servant of the Lord," "Son of Man," "Last Adam"—all the titles applied to him are "corporate" terms. They all imply a person in whom the race is somehow incorporated and by

whom it is represented. Jesus saw his mission (and we should see it) as bound
to our destiny. If he was not raised, there is no hope, but if he was raised, it
spells resurrection and redemption for the world.[3]

The resurrection means not only that Jesus' pre-Easter claims were vindi-
cated, but also that a new age and the possibility of redemption had opened
up for all people. The resurrection spells life from the dead for humanity
and new creation. The resurrection not only validated his claims to be God's
Son but also signified the end of fallen history and the beginning of the new
age. As our representative, Jesus was firstborn from death among many
brothers and sisters and the firstfruits of those who sleep in death. Peter
called him "the Author of life" for this very reason (Acts 3:15). If Jesus is alive,
there is hope for the world and life beyond death.[4]

The book of Hebrews states that it was fitting for God to become a human
being (2:10-11). The author finds it appropriate that God should have
endured pain and suffering in the person of Christ, experienced temptation
as we do and triumphed over death for our sakes. Making corporate assump-
tions, the early Greek theology often stated that humanity, if it was to be
healed, had to be assumed by God and its wounds healed in him. God had
to assume the broken life that was to be healed and had to endure death and
resurrection in our place. For this reason Jesus endured suffering and was
exalted at God's right hand, sending forth a signal that the new creation had
begun.

Easter also underwrote the necessity of world mission, since everyone
everywhere must now be told and enabled to participate in what has been
done for them. By highlighting the resurrection, the Christian message
promises the coming of the kingdom of God, whereby humanity will experience redemption at the end of history. The resurrection of Jesus is the
pledge and foretaste of this event and gives hope and an answer to death.[5]

The Problem of the Courtroom Model

How was it that the cross became more central than the resurrection in
Western theology? Why is it more common to hear people ascribe redemptive value to the cross than to the resurrection? Why is the resurrection so
grossly neglected in our systematic theologies as compared to the atonement?[6]

The explanation, we believe, lies in the legal orientation of Western
theology, which does not leave room for the resurrection to have saving

value. Think of it: If the human problem is essentially one of guilt rather than death, and if the solution is primarily the satisfaction of the cross, what place is left for the resurrection to have saving value? Once Christ died and sin is atoned for, the legal problem is solved; what else is there to solve? In this scenario the resurrection is mainly icing on the cake and not a main event.

The corrective to this lies in seeing that Christ is our representative and substitute in a much larger sense. Not just in death, but in his life, death and resurrection, Jesus stood in the place of lost humanity. From beginning to end, his whole experience of incarnation was a grand substitution. He lived and died and rose again vicariously. Paul puts it succinctly when he says that "one has died for all; therefore all have died" (2 Cor 5:14). He means that humanity died in Jesus' death and humanity rises in his life, because he represents it. The human problem is larger than guilt, and the solution is broader than the cross.

Is Death the End?

We ought to be glad that our faith features resurrection. After all, death is a fundamental problem, and religion, to be credible, needs an answer for it. Is death the end? Do we face annihilation of possibilities? Does life end in absurdity? Is death the end of a meaningless life?

It is hard to believe that death is the end for two reasons. First, there is what C. S. Lewis calls an inconsolable longing in us for something more, a voice inside telling us that death is not the end. Why do we feel this way? Why do we have a thirst that nothing in this world can quench? Why do we feel there is Someone calling to us? This desire, we believe, points to the fact that we were made for something more than death, as the gospel declares.

Second, it is hard to believe that death is the end because of our hope for final justice. Few people find fulfillment in this earthly life. Most have lived under difficult circumstances, with their potential unrealized. Life is very unsatisfactory indeed if death is the end of everything. Most people die before being fully born. Life is indeed tragic if it concludes in death. We need a vision such as the resurrection gives us, where good is brought out of evil in the end. This is a vision we can really live with. It tells us that human existence is not a limitless tragedy but is destined for a good fulfillment beyond death. The only way for there to be a final righting of wrongs is for

there to be life beyond this one. This we can believe if we accept the good
news of resurrection.[7]

What Does Resurrection Signify?

But it would be a misunderstanding to construe the promise of everlasting
life as a bribe to induce us to love God. This may explain why God did not
reveal it clearly to Israel. Though there are hints of life beyond death in the
Old Testament, Israel had to love God without really knowing the full extent
of what God had prepared for his beloved. Christians should love God for
his own sake, even if everlasting life were not part of the gospel package.

Everlasting life, even when its promise is known, cannot be a bribe because
of its nature. There is nothing about it that a mercenary person could desire.
It is not at all like winning a lottery, for example. Heaven is a place where
love for God is consummated. As marriage for lovers is a prize related to love,
heaven for believers is intrinsic to their faith. It is a situation in which our
feeble love for God can be fulfilled. Only a person who loves God on earth
already would want to be in heaven. Perhaps the reason Jesus said only the
pure in heart would see God was that they are the only ones who would want
to. Anyone else would be uncomfortable.

Heaven represents the possibility of loving God more than we now do. It
would be desirable only for persons who want more of that opportunity. If a
person did not want it, heaven would be like hell.

Another misunderstanding of the Christian hope has to do with other-
worldliness. Does our hope undercut commitment to good causes here on
earth? The reason this is not a problem is that hope for resurrection is hope
for the redemption of the world as created and loved by God. Belief in
resurrection thus reinforces and does not negate commitment to the creation. It makes such commitment very important. Atheism inevitably undercuts commitment to the world, because it argues that there is finally nothing
of value or meaning in the world. Christian hope, on the other hand, spurs
us to commitment to our world and the people in it.

C. S. Lewis once said that because we love something beyond the world,
we are able to love the world better than those who have nothing else. Loving
God is a solid basis for loving the creation, because God is its Creator and
Redeemer. Hope for perfected humanity in the presence of the triune God
beyond death has positive implications for action in this earthly life. It lets
us live in hope in the midst of despair, and it tells us that love, sharing and

cohumanity are matters of ultimate significance.

The resurrection of Jesus is the foretaste of the resurrection of the dead, and this hope is a strong basis of meaningful social and individual life on the earth. People who hope do more for this world than those without hope. As Lewis said, "Aim at heaven and you will get the earth thrown in; aim at earth and you will get neither."[8] Hope for resurrection sustains a committed life in this world and points us forward to a new creation, not just of individuals but of humanity itself.

What Will Resurrection Be Like?

Because the descriptions of the new creation in the Bible refer to matters that are outside our present experience and beyond our imaginations, they are necessarily symbolic. One can only use language from this side of death to refer to that which lies beyond it. Resurrection itself is a metaphor of awakening from the sleep of death, waking up to an altogether new reality. We are going to see things that no eye has ever seen, things that we can only express by symbols because they are beyond present experience.

Gold, for example, is a good symbol for life in eternity because it is has value and never rusts. Crowns speak of royal splendor, while musical instruments express ecstasy and joy. Reality will surpass all these things, but the symbols give us an inkling. Everlasting life is life made completely whole, where the effects of sin will be no more and where pain, sorrow and death will perish. In this restoration we will become all we were meant to be and will inhabit a renewed creation. The world will be bathed in light, and God will be fully present.

The image of resurrection suggests that we will have a more perfect body, one that will express personality and relate to others in new ways. The idea of spending eternity as a disembodied soul is not appealing, but in the Apostles' Creed we confess *the resurrection of the body*, not the survival of disembodied souls. We look forward not to the immortality of the soul but to the resurrection of the whole person.[9]

Hope for the consummation of history beyond the world is deeply meaningful when symbolized in the image of resurrection. The re-creation of a person in body and soul is a meaningful idea, not an illogical one. The Bible and modern anthropology agree that body and soul go together as a unit, that body and soul form a personal whole. A credible hope, then, must involve a resurrection of the whole person.

One way to think of this is to imagine God replicating a dead person in another place. Imagine John Brown dying in Canada and turning up the next day in China. The fellow is an exact replica of the dead man, with the same physical and mental characteristics. He even says he is John Brown. It is as if he had been re-created in another place as a fully embodied human person. This is thinkable if you grant that there is a God powerful enough to do such a thing. And who can deny that the God who made the world is able to fulfill such purposes for humankind?[10]

An atheist might counter that resurrection is an impossibility because there is no God to raise the dead. This is true (and so much the worse) for the atheistic model. In creative love theism, the divine Artist, having designed us in the first place, has the wisdom and power to resurrect us to improved bodies appropriate for a new creation. The argument between atheist and theist about resurrection lies in a difference of models and presuppositions and has little to do with scientific fact.

One difficulty with a replica model of the resurrection is the fact that it posits no physical continuity between the body of earthly life and the resurrected body. It suggests a new body materially unrelated to the old, a new one expressing our personality in a new environment. Many theologians have held that there must be some continuity of particles between the two bodies. This is difficult to imagine and would not be strictly necessary, since the cells of our body change every seven years.

The reason theologians insist on some material continuity is the fact that Jesus rose bodily, and the impression Paul gives is that the old body is transformed into a new one, not replaced. The issue probably comes down to the fact that resurrection as the firstfruits of a renewal of the whole creation must not be seen as replacement but as transformation. To ease our minds we could say that there will be material continuity of some kind, but we cannot say exactly of what kind.

Resurrection Life
What aspects of earthly life would we expect to continue and expand after the resurrection? Creative love theism suggests some possible answers arising out of its vision of God as primarily loving parent. Loving parents on earth want their children to be able to crawl, to walk, to run and eventually to drive and be free to travel. By analogy, we are sure that God will make it possible for us to grow more in our friendship with him. We imagine that the

resurrection will enable us to meet and relate to people of all nations and times. We will watch as all the nations bring their cultural treasures into the heavenly city. We will all be able to visit, communicate with and enjoy each other on a vast scale.

Loving parents on earth want their children to be creative, form words, string them into sentences, tell stories, write stories, paint pictures, write poems, learn music, make quilts, garden and so on. But in life we are continually frustrated by limitations of creativity based in mortality. God wants us to be free to enjoy the language of heaven, to write and paint, to dance and compose and sing melodies with all possible accompaniments.

Loving parents on earth in particular want their children to be free to love. In this body we long to know and be known, to love and be loved, but our loving is restrained and made difficult beyond the few persons whom we trust. Since God loves us and wants us to love, we can imagine our great Lover giving us bodies capable of loving to a fuller extent. In this life we have intimations and glimpses of what perfect loving might be like, but much more lies ahead.

God will surely satisfy the longings of the human heart. One frustration in life is that from time to time we have a vision of a beauty that we would love to create, a joy that we would love to enjoy, a love that we would love to enter. The paraplegic longs to walk and run, swim and climb mountains, dance ecstatically with abandon. The deaf long to hear, the blind to see. Atheists may suppose such longings are futile, but Christian hope enables us to picture every longing being satisfied and nothing good being lost. In heaven there will be the time and opportunity needed to capture and recapture the longings, the beauty, the joy, and to see a fulfillment to all that this life has left unsatisfied. The pleasure will be multiplied in the knowledge that every other person is finding his or her satisfaction too.

We cannot prove that all this will be the case. But we can picture possibilities and dream of what resurrection might mean. Whatever pictures we use are metaphorical, based on what we can now experience in our world. But we know, because God is truly loving, that the reality will not be less than these pictures but will surpass them.

Most essentially, life in the kingdom of God will involve interpersonal fellowship with the persons of the Trinity. It is not the life of the solitary self, but life in community with God and others. As on earth we are social beings and exist in relationship with other persons, so in heaven we will grow in this dimension. We will more and more transcend an individualist orientation and grow in our capacity for relationships. There will be an experience of community beyond anything we know now. As we grow in our knowledge of the God who incorporates three personal centers that relate to one another in loving relationships, we will find fulfillment in a communion that reflects that love flowing from God the Trinity. The many persons in heaven will not exist over against one another, but rather with one another and in openness to one another.

When asked a question about a woman who had lived with seven brothers in succession, Jesus commented, "In the resurrection they neither marry nor are given in marriage, but are like angels in heaven" (Mt 22:30). He also chastised his interrogators for not realizing that Abraham, Isaac and Jacob would be not less alive but more alive on the other side of death, because their relationship with God could not be destroyed by death. All others who love God will also live beyond death, thanks to his grace and power. Human beings matter to God, and he will not see them scrapped.

Centuries ago Pascal offered a wager to help people decide about the truth of the gospel. He said that it made sense to accept it because if it proves true, one will have gained everything, and if it is not true, nothing will have been lost. In creative love theism, too, there is nothing to lose. God has already included us in salvation without our asking. We have been accepted into the life and love of God. Unconditional love gives us freedom and fosters our own ability to love. The light of the resurrection calls us to a love that makes life full and fulfilling. Faith is a risk, but it is better to bet on life than fall into despair.

Jesus Christ has brought a new order into being. Lives can be changed, hearts made new, bodies healed because our human nature has been raised in him. The Risen One gives us a glimpse of real life without limitations for all eternity in the kingdom of God. The whole creation now is feeling the birth pangs of newness.

IV

TRINITY
Personal
Love

GOD IS LOVE, AND GOD INVITES HUMANITY INTO A LOVING FAMILY FELLOW-
ship. The doctrine of the Trinity fits this idea perfectly. God is not like a
solitary person but like a society of persons. The gospel declares God to be
a fellowship of the Father, Son and Spirit in the unity of one essence,
essentially a fellowship of loving mutual relationships.

Love, then, is not just something that God decides to do, not just an
occasional attribute. Loving is what characterizes God essentially—as a
dynamic livingness, a divine circling and relating. God is not a solitary
monarch but a tripersonal mystery of love. God is a fellowship of persons, a
relational being, open to the joy and pain of the world. This model of God
in Christian faith helps us understand the purpose of creation. God creates
in order to create love and relationships, because he delights to hear in the
love of finite persons an echo of the love that constitutes his own reality.[1]

How do we know this about God? We know it because this is what has been
revealed in the history of Israel and in the event of Jesus Christ. It captures
the heart of the biblical revelation of God's redemptive activities in the world.
It is an inference drawn from the incarnation and the outpoured Spirit. As
we see the Father, Son and Spirit relating mutually and lovingly with one

another in the history of salvation, we learn that God is a social trinity. Jesus
is differentiated from Father and Spirit while sharing deity with them. Father
and Son are not just metaphors of an earthly relationship—these names
point to an eternal relationship that together with the Spirit constitutes a
threefoldness in God. For this reason we are baptized in the name of Father,
Son and Spirit, three centers of divine personality and activity (Mt 28:19).
This is why Paul speaks of receiving love from the Father, grace from Jesus
Christ and fellowship in the Spirit (2 Cor 13:13). Salvation has a triune
structure: we have been chosen by the Father, redeemed by the Son and
sealed by the Spirit (Eph 1:3-14).[2]

The Unsolitary God

Such triadic speech employed in describing God represents a very special
kind of monotheism. God is not seen as a solitary power but as the epitome
of costly love that renews life. The Trinity is the God who grounds other-
affirming love, for whom giving and receiving love is of the essence. God is
not a distant monarch, a supreme will to power, but One whose being is to
give and receive love. It follows that God's will is for community in which
power and love are shared, where love and not compulsion reigns.[3]

Daniel Migliore comments: "God is not absolute power, not infinite
egocentrism, not majestic solitariness. The power of the triune God is not
coercive but creative, sacrificial, and empowering love. The glory of the
triune God consists not in dominating others but in sharing life with others."[4]

The doctrine of the Trinity defines the goal of salvation as being part of
the divine fellowship, participating in the loving interaction of the Trinity.
No legal model can capture this. Of course we need to be forgiven of our
sins, but pardon is only a first step along a path to the real goal: fellowship
with the triune God. Human beings are social creatures, made for mutuality,
cooperation and interaction with one another. We are made not just human
but *cohuman*, designed for communion, called into the fellowship of the
triune God. Thus the Bible speaks of our being summoned to a banquet,
called to life in a new city, gathered together in a great throng—the goal is
oneness with others and union with God.

The Trinity signals relational fullness and a richness of being in God. It
depicts God as an open and dynamic structure, the essence of loving
community. Atheism rejects God as the enemy of human freedom because
God has been presented as an alienating solitary Ego. But this is a caricature

of the truth. God is not the enemy of human freedom but its very ground and support. God is for us, not against us. God seeks our wholeness and delights in doing us good.

The Trinity means that God, though self-sufficient in divine fullness, is capable of creating and opening up to creation in overflowing love. Though he does not strictly need the world, he loves it. As a relational being, God delights to invite creatures into fellowship. He has created a dynamic world with real value out of the abundance of his own inner richness. It delighted God to make a world like ours, a world with free agents, capable of choice, because this is the sort of world in which loving community can occur, a world that can echo back God's own social life. To make such a world was risky, but this world is a place that brings pleasure to God—a world not wholly determined by him, but one that can provide occasions of meaningful interaction and involvement.

Under no necessity to do so, God freely created a world with real significance and accepted the risks involved in entering into relationship with it. Genesis says God found the creation good because God is dynamic and open. He loves a creation that is open like this one. The Trinity can be likened to a dance that expresses itself by inviting others to join in as new partners. This is what the Greek theologians meant when they declared "deification" to be the goal of human life.

As personal life in relationship, God is eager to enter into loving relationships with us. God is faithful Father, serving Son and enlivening Spirit. Himself existing in community, God wants to establish community among us. Church and family can be expressions of God's nature, of his love of open friendships, caring relationships and inclusive communities. God is the power of a self-giving love that will prove stronger than even sin and death. When Paul says, "God's foolishness is wiser than human wisdom" (1 Cor 1:25), he means that God takes the apparently foolish path leading to suffering and death for the sake of our salvation. Only a triune God who treasures other-regarding love would think of such a strategy.

We believe in one God who is not solitary but a loving communion marked by overflowing life. What stands at the center of the universe is shared life. As perfect sociality, God embodies qualities of mutuality, reciprocity, cooperation and peace. This identity as triune is fundamental to creative love theism. It underlies its major concerns: God is inclusive love, more loving parent than judge, open mutuality rather than all-determining. The Trinity

captures the vision of creative love theism. God's will from the foundation
of the world has been to share his life with the human race in community.

A Rational Conundrum

This may be biblical and theologically inspiring, but does it make sense? Is
it not a contradiction to say God is one (in essence) but three (in person)?
No, it is not a contradiction or merely a puzzle. Outside mathematics, where
1 equals 1, most entities are far from numerically simple. Is an atom simple?
Is an organism simple? Is a human being simple? The higher the form of an
entity, it seems, the more complex its unity. Only in math is oneness simple.
In most other areas, unity and complexity coexist. This is true of God, who
is complex oneness and a society of three distinct but associated persons in
mysterious relationship.

To see the rationality, compare the triune and unitarian models. How can
God be personal and loving without being triune? How would personality
and love be expressed before creation in the absence of any world? A
unitarian-type God would need a world to fight off loneliness and to express
a loving and personal nature. It would be necessary to create a world in order
to solve God's inner deficiencies. A triune God, on the other hand, could
create a universe and love it for its own sake, not because he needed it.
Creation would be an overflow of his loving, not a necessity.

So the trinity model makes God free in his creation of the world. Though
often criticized as a conundrum, the Trinity seems actually to be rationally
superior to the alternatives.

The Eternal Conversation

The doctrine makes practical sense as well.[5] It sanctifies loving social relations between humans, since these are grounded in and mirror interactions
within the Trinity. Relating to one another in family, church and society can
be a reflection of God's own social nature. The divine society is mirrored in
the bondedness of our own loving relationships, because God is the essence
of other-regarding love.

The Hebrew word for God is a plural noun. Whatever the reason for this
in antiquity, for us it hints at God's being social and communicative. Language too is an important vehicle of loving relations. The Bible opens with
an account of loving communication. Its record of the conversation begins
as God says, "Let there be light." It continues as names are given to day and

night, sky, land and sea. At each stage God steps back and says: "Yes, this is good." This part of the conversation draws to a close with "Let us make humankind in our image, according to our likeness." The verb here is plural, indicating a plurality in God. And the creatures here are social beings, and from the moment of creation they are addressed in language about their calling to love, worship and obey God.

The social Trinity, then, is the picture of an eternal conversation that issues in a world where humans engage in conversation with one another and join in the conversation that God has initiated. The second chapter of Genesis depicts the beginning of a conversation between men and women, who are partners with God and one another in the grace of life. Despite human failure and betrayal, the story of salvation goes on depicting God as continually seeking to bring sinners back into the conversation. The story ends in the new creation as an expanded, loving conversation between God and people from all nations.

The doctrine of the Trinity is an essential part of creative love theism. If God's very nature is love, then God was love before the creation of human beings. And since it is impossible to love when one is alone, in order for love to be possible, God's being must have a structure that permits it. It requires the sort of plurality of persons in the single divine nature which the Christian revelation discloses.

The Trinity is an offense to Muslims and to Jews. The oneness of God is the first requirement of their creed. They criticize Christian faith for appearing to suggest the existence of three gods. We agree with them about the importance of God's oneness—that is not in question. The issue is whether the oneness of God allows inner relationships or not. As already noted, in many fields such as physics and biology oneness allows the unity of several constituents in relationship. Scientists picture the single atom as having an inner complexity. Their model for an atom of helium is a society of entities— proton, neutron and electron held together by atomic force. The inner constituents and relationships of the oneness of uranium are even more complex. And the oneness of a simple cell involves a large number of interrelationships. So the quarrel between unitarian and trinitarian theism is really about the kind of oneness there is in God. In the trinitarian model the unity of God is a unity of persons bound by love and involved in conversation.

With loving personal conversation and fellowship with God central to our model, an element of process is introduced. God is not impassive but cares deeply for us. God listens, responds, delights, weeps, is grieved. The difficulty with classical theism, so influenced by Hellenism, is that it makes God impassive and unable to relate. It removes God from the process of real involvement with the world and makes it hard to envisage real conversation with the three persons of the Trinity. The narrative of the Bible does not leave the impression of immutability or impassivity on God's part. The Trinity is a lively picture of God. The love that flows within God also flows out to the world and becomes involved in all of its joys and sorrows.

The Greek fathers offer a distinctive way of picturing the inner life of God. They imagine an eternal, loving dance in the unity of the life of the Trinity. The function of the liturgy, in turn, is to embody this interactive oneness within God and call every human being to join in this fellowship and conversation. We are called to give ourselves over to God and abide in God without losing our identity.

Metaphors of Three Persons
Given the trinitarian logic of our model, let's inquire into our language in relation to the three persons. We do not have access to God's essence—what we can say about God is by way of the metaphors of revelation. There are hundreds of metaphors used in the Bible to talk about God, and together they help us get a picture of the divine nature.

One area of difficulty today is gender terms. The traditional way of speaking of God makes it sound as if God were a male. This is because we have given preference to masculine images for God and allowed female images in the Bible to go largely unretrieved. But God is not a sexual being; he is neither male nor female. So we need to be careful not to suggest that he is. The solution cannot be to stop using personal language for God, because God is personal, not impersonal—someone, not something. We could speak of the Spirit in female terms to create a better gender balance. This is easy, since the Bible imputes feminine-type activities to the Spirit, such as comforting and giving birth. A better solution, however, is to recognize that male *and* female images are used in the Bible for each and every person in the Trinity. God is a father who cares for us (Ps 103:13) and a mother who gives birth and defends us (Is 49:15). Jesus was incarnated as a male, but does not make his masculinity an issue; he embodies Wisdom from the Old Testament. The Spirit is both a mighty wind and a life-giver in creation and new creation—a well of life, nourishing and consoling, sympathizing and empathizing. The thing is not to absolutize our language but strive always to enrich our way of speaking with the entire biblical range of metaphors. Let us enrich existing expressions by adding others, without losing anything valuable. We can complement the traditional images rather than replacing them.

Viewing God as personal means that we cannot avoid the issue of gender. The mystery of God transcends male and female. Since God created male and female in his image, either male or female images can be used to point to God. We must learn to use neglected female images of God without embarrassment alongside the images we have been using. The strategy is one of addition, not subtraction or reversal.

When Christians interact with God, the conversation goes along several lines. We converse with God as parent, as friend and as Spirit. We may feel like a little child crying out to God for comfort or protection. We may talk to God as our friend who walks with us and loves us. Or we may speak to the Spirit at work within us to give us wisdom and strength. We deal in our Christian experience with all three persons of the Trinity.

The Person of the Spirit
The Spirit is the powerful wind of God that moves upon the waters. The Hebrew word speaks of vitality, vibrancy and movement. The Spirit is the life-giver, divine energy, in creation and in new creation. It is God in action in the cosmos and in human life. The Spirit is not confined to any structures, but blows wherever it wills. The Spirit everywhere comes to the rescue of humankind, causing the earth to flourish and love to abound, opening up schools of mercy wherever possible.[6]

The basic metaphor of wind suggests a power moving us like a sailing ship and lifting us like an eagle. It is the power of God that moved judges like Deborah and Gideon. It is a term for the air we breathe, suggesting images of inspiration and anointing. It is said of Bezalel, an artist in the building of the tabernacle, that he was empowered by the Spirit to do his work (Ex 31:2-3). Prophets like Isaiah were inspired to rebuke injustice and explain visions of God. David was anointed in composing and singing psalms. The Spirit enables us to ride the wind like eagles effortlessly gliding in the sky for hours, letting the wind do the work.

In addition to the image of the wind and of breathing, there are metaphors of fire and water. Winds blow and fires burn in different modes. They may be violent or quiet, raging or warming. The work of the Spirit is like water poured out in the desert. The Spirit is a friend called alongside to help us, our Comforter.

In some theology it is said that the Spirit is present and active only where persons have repented and believed in Jesus. But this is to ignore the fact that the Spirit goes before Christ to prepare the way for him. The Spirit is present everywhere in the world and active (as the Old Testament shows) among people not yet Christian. Samson knew nothing about Christ and was not a particularly holy man, yet he was stirred by the Spirit of the Lord. The Spirit was at work in an Arabian like Job. We must not place limits on the Spirit, who is at work in the whole world and not just in our domain.

The Person of the Son

The love of God for the world takes public form in Jesus Christ. In him the glory of God blazes forth into the world. Risen from the dead, he is the proof of the truth and goodness of God. Through the Spirit he stands before every heart and asks to enter.

Because the Trinity is eternal, we do not limit the work of the Logos just to the events of Jesus' life. The Spirit enables the Son to be preexperienced as the friend beside us before the New Testament gospel comes on the scene. He visits and intervenes in the history of every nation.

The second person was born as a male human being. No doubt there were circumstances that made this appropriate. But that does not make the essence of the Logos male, any more than it is Jewish or Galilean. The important thing is that the Word became *flesh*, not that it became male. "Son of God" itself is a metaphor, pointing to a social relationship with God; it is not a statement about gender. It would be a radical distortion to depict the incarnation as supporting patriarchalism when its outcome is deliverance from all forms of oppression. Jesus is God's Child who seeks the wholeness and full humanity of everyone. He summons men and women to a community where there is neither male nor female.

When the Logos was born among us, we see him touching, loving, conversing, healing, walking, turning the other cheek and letting himself be sacrificed. He did not begin to do those things only when he came among us in the flesh. There are many references in the Old Testament to God's engaging in the same activities that are familiar to us from the life of Jesus.

Each one of these visitations and interventions points to the second person's coming into personal contact with humans. Christ was present when God walked with Adam in the garden and was with the Hebrew youth in the fiery furnace. The second person is spoken of in the paradoxical metaphors of Lord and servant, shepherd and lamb, lion and child. These images used by the prophets are picked up by the New Testament writers. C. S. Lewis captured such metaphors effectively in his picture of Aslan in the Narnia stories. Servant and Lord, lion and child, shepherd, helper and lamb picture various aspects of the strength and gentleness of this person. What a different view of power he gives us! Jesus said,

> You know that the rulers of the Gentiles lord it over them, and their great ones are tyrants over them. It will not be so among you; but whoever wishes to be great among you must be your servant, and whoever wishes to be first among you must be your slave; just as the Son of Man came not to be served but to serve, and to give his life a ransom for many. (Mt 20:25-28)

Jesus does not seek power over people. Love is the shape power comes in. This power is the strength that enables the loved one to mature and that inspires people to speak out for justice. This is a power that does not sap but fosters life in the other person. It is a love that bonds and empowers. God-power does not want to dominate—it wants to persuade and build up. The power of the cross is not about a payment but about freedom from sin and death. A servant ministry is always concerned about the freedom of others.

The Person of Father

God is present and at work in every sphere of creation through the Spirit. He is at work in the whole world, upholding and gracing. We dwell in the one world of the one Lord. The divine mystery that surrounds us calls us to love and right living between all peoples.

There are metaphors of God's mothering as well as fathering in the Bible (Deut 14:1; 32:6; Ps 10:14, 18; 68:5; 89:26; 131:2; Is 49:15; 66:13). God ministers to us in the capacity of both parents. When we call out to God like a child crying for its parents, God is there. This is true for anyone anywhere. God does not make people wait until Christ comes on the scene. The Father is not niggardly, refusing to respond to someone who cries out to him using the wrong name. A loving parent respond to any name his or her children use in their need. God looks to the heart, not to outward appearances.

The Trinity is not divided—God is three persons united by love. When you enter conversation with the Father, the Son is at your side and the Spirit is interceding in the depth of your being. Some people may begin by talking to the Father and only later learn to talk to the Son or to the Spirit. Others may first learn to call on the Spirit. For many others, hearing the stories of Jesus and picturing him as a friend has been the way for them to enter a conversation with God. People can enter into conversation with God in many ways.

The triune God is a mystery, but fortunately, understanding is not a prerequisite for knowing God. What needs to be held out to the whole world is that a wonderful divine love calls to every person to enter into fellowship with God and a new humanity in the new creation.

PART TWO
Doctrine
of
Sin

W HAT A RELIGION BELIEVES IS WRONG WITH HUMANITY, WHAT IT THINKS stands in the way of reaching salvation, constitutes its doctrine of sin. One needs to know what has gone wrong in order to know how to correct it. Having discussed the goal of humanity as fellowship with God, we turn in part two to a diagnosis of what hinders us and consider the nature of divine judgment on sin.

In creative love theism, sin is not defined primarily as a legal infraction or in terms of transgressions that require punishment. Sin is a mysterious refusal to accept God's love (chapter five). God responds to this rejection with judgments suitable to the situation but, like the father of the prodigal, remains unwilling that any should perish. Therefore God's work of judgment is aimed at restoration of relationships, not at rejection (chapter six). Similarly, the Second Coming of Christ is not a final doomsday but the climax of a series of comings in history aimed at restoration (chapter seven). But since it is possible for sinners to remain stubbornly impenitent and to reject God's love finally, we must also discuss hell (chapter eight).

V

DIAGNOSIS
Defective
Love

WHAT IS IT THAT KEEPS PEOPLE FROM SALVATION? A RELIGION WITH A LEGAL framework will interpret sin in a moral way, as a transgression of precepts. Religions that stress lack of knowledge as the problem will define sin in terms of mistaken beliefs. Where religion is understood as a personal encounter, however, sin will be seen as what spoils the relationship, causing alienation and estrangement. In creative love theism, sin is a rejection of God's love and a turning away from his gracious presence. In a broader sense, sin is the power that obstructs God's plan to make things new, the power that enslaves reality under the dominion of death.[1]

Image Broken
The best way to understand sin is to define it against the backdrop of what humanity was made to be. Sin is what frustrates God's purpose for us.[2] First of all, to be in God's image is to have the capacity for a personal relationship with God, to enjoy the freedom to respond to God. He wants us to respond to his grace in every area of life.[3]

Second, there is the fact that we humans are social and relational beings, that we find our identity in coexistence with one another before God, not in isolation. Our freedom is meant to be exercised not in isolation from others but in interaction. We are created for life in community, for relationships of mutual fidelity. In this way we are to image the triune God, who delights in love and community.

Third, being in God's image is not a static condition but a calling with a goal. Genesis tells us that it involves exercising stewardly dominion over the world and taking responsibility for unfolding history. As people of destiny, then, we feel restless for a fulfillment of our lives and look to the unrealized future. We are creatures of hope, open to what is coming, in dynamic partnership with God, looking for the kingdom of God.

This positive picture of human nature and what it is meant to be helps us understand the meaning of sin. Sin reverses and distorts what we are meant to be. The disorder of human life is visible in brutality and deceit and in the alienation and oppression that characterize the human condition. The created structures of humanity have been disrupted on every level.

Relationship Broken
First, sin tries to deny the relationship with God that we were created for and to hide our need for divine grace. Sin says no to the call of God. It is a refusal to serve God and live gratefully before him. Sin is not primarily lawbreaking or a code violation (serious though that is), but a rejection of God and his love for us. It may take many forms: it may take the form of pride, in which we declare ourselves to be gods in place of God, or it may take the form of sloth and self-rejection, a refusal to accept the challenge of life with God.

Second, sin distorts proper social relationships among us. It is not only the refusal to live before God but a refusal to live with and for our neighbors. This underlies the specific transgressions against them. At this level too, sin takes different forms. In the folly of self-exaltation one can seek to have power over and dominate others; or in acts of self-destruction one may give up and slide into powerlessness. In either case our humanity is damaged, whether by lording it over others or by failing to resist being oppressed and just giving up.

Third, sin refuses our destiny in its refusal to be open to God's coming kingdom. This refusal may take the form of either resignation or presumption. It can manifest itself in an attempt to bring in the kingdom without God due to confidence in ourselves and our goodness, or it may take the form of forsaking the promise of the kingdom and throwing in the towel.

Either way we close ourselves off from the future to which God points us.

We believe it is a mistake to think of sin primarily as the violation of a code, because it is more than that. Sin is the disruption of our relationship with God. This is well illustrated in David's experience recorded in Psalm 51. The Bible tells the story of how he possessed Bathsheba by getting her husband killed in battle. Without doubt that is a violation of the commandments, but that aspect is not mentioned in the psalm. Without mentioning Bathsheba, David confesses: "Against you [God], you alone, have I sinned" (Ps 51:4). Though it was certainly wrong to have treated Uriah and Bathsheba as David did, the offense was ultimately against God himself. Breaking rules is wrong, but breaking relationship is worse.

Because God is love, sin should be understood essentially as a refusal of love. Made for relationship, humans have the ability to accept or refuse that. The meaning of the fall into sin is that instead of trusting God and finding security in him, the couple try to find it in themselves. It seems that the decision to create human beings was a risky thing for God to do. Making a creature capable of love meant creating a person with the possibility of either receiving or refusing love. The possibility exists for such a person to give love to something or someone for which that love was not intended. Evidently God wanted us to love him freely—without freedom, love could not be genuine. As it happens, we employed our freedom to serve selfishness and pride and chose a self-destructive independence.

Sin is the refusal to anchor ourselves in God and find our security in him. It is the decision to misuse the gift of freedom and disrupt the created structures of existence, leading to alienation and disorder. Sin tries to deny our relatedness to God and our need of his grace. It is the refusal to live in the service of God and in friendship with our fellow creatures. Not so much the violation of a moral code, sin is the disruption of the relationship for which we were made.

Breaking that relationship not only caused us grief, but it also brought great pain to God. God's is the pain of a lover who calls but receives no answer. Listen to the pain in Jesus' lament: "Jerusalem, Jerusalem, the city that kills the prophets and stones those who are sent to it! How often have I desired to gather your children together as a hen gathers her brood under her wings, and you were not willing!" (Mt 23:37). Isaiah describes God's sorrow in these terms:

I was ready to be sought out by those who did not ask,

to be found by those who did not seek me.

I said, "Here I am, here I am,"

to a nation that did not call on my name." (Is 65:1)

In Hosea, too, God asks himself what he can do with his people in the face of this betrayal (Hosea 11:8). What will it take to put things right?

In the cross we see what sin is in its essence, and what the remedy has to be. The death of Jesus shows both what sinners are prepared to do when God comes to them and what God is prepared to do to save his ungodly enemies. In putting Jesus to death, sinners revealed how far they are willing to go to be gods themselves. This act, more than any other, reveals what a self-enclosed life really means. This is a life that wastes opportunity and falls into inhumanity and dissolution. At the cross we see sinners just like ourselves putting to death a man completely committed to the cause of men and women.

Sin is the rejection of God's love and of God's will for the world. It is a rejection of what we were created for, the rejection of a dynamic relationship with God. The judgment of God must blaze against it, but this is really the response of a rejected lover, not judicial condemnation.

Explaining Sin

What is the reason for the awful wrongness at the heart of human life? Doctrines of original sin are not uncommon today, even among secularists, because it is obvious that life is not now what it was meant to be. One does not have to believe in God to sense that something is terribly wrong and to see the need to account for it.

Karl Marx conjectured that humans must first have lived in harmony with one another before the class distinctions that produce alienation appeared. In this paradise lost, humankind was once innocent (he surmised), free of exploitation, but by reason of some dark error we fell from grace. Sigmund Freud, for his part, posited an archetypal memory of humanity in its prime, from which it has fallen. Claude Lévi-Strauss imagined a transition from a natural state to a cultural one that has left humanity scarred. He views the theft of fire from the gods (that is, technology) as leading to the tragedies of civilization.

All three of these secularists happen to be Jews, and one hears echoes of biblical thinking in their musings. Each is trying to explain some breach of covenant with creation which produced humanity's present predicament.

All are trying to replace theology with a mythology of their own.

In religions too there are doctrines of original sin. Buddhists believe that sin originates when we begin to desire things, while monists view ignorance as the basic mistake. In Christian theology, original sin is pictured in the story of Adam and Eve eating the forbidden fruit in the Garden of Eden. In this story we are able to reflect on our own lives and discover at the depth of our being the same temptation to pride or despair and to destructive independence. But how did this one decision produce a corporate result such that the whole race is inclined to sin? The Bible does not explain how this happened, though we can try to tease out something. Scripture is more practical than speculative, more inclined to speak of the reality of sin, the need of repentance and the promise of redemption than to supply explanations. We might say that the Bible is more interested in the exodus of sin than in its genesis, more oriented to a victory over sin than to explaining its origins.

But the Bible does present sin both as a universal condition and as a chosen act for which persons are responsible.[4] It sees sin as both the corruption of individuals and an active power in corporate structures.

Also, the fact that we are social beings helps us see that our actions affect others and not just ourselves. Decisions have social and corporate effects; they are more than isolated individual decisions. They may have a social, even racial, impact. Think of individual birds in a flock. Each is flying on its own, but they all turn together as if their movement were orchestrated. Similarly, we have all witnessed crowds of individuals lusting for blood or cheering their sports team on. We have been pained to see what tribes do to one another in acts of cruelty that hardly a person among them would even consider on his or her own. The concept of original sin is in touch with deep realities well known to us.

We are able to conceive of Adam's decision to turn away from God as a decision that became more than an occasional act of his own: a decision that has come to characterize humanity as a whole. Original sin refers to a mysterious self-disposing away from the divine call, a disposition that marks humanity as a whole. Though we are many, we are also one. Humanity in Adam made this fateful decision in its collective heart and soul.

To some extent we can see how this works out in terms of the influence our decisions can have on one another. Few of our sins are completely private choices—they often affect others. In its account of the Fall, the Bible tells us that something has gone wrong with humanity as a whole. This is a profound insight, even if we cannot know the precise mechanism.[5]

It makes sense to think of the Fall as being historical. There must have been a moment when the decision was first taken and the new direction was first chosen. Depravity is not natural but must have begun at some point, though we cannot date it. Such a turning point would have had to be posited had the Bible not reported it.

Freedom and Responsibility

As for individual moral responsibility in a social context such as this, we see each person as being sucked into the vortex of a damaging historical process. There is a tragic dimension to this: they cannot prevent it from happening to them. But we should not think of them as personally responsible for the sin of the ancestors, but only responsible for their own deeds. Ezekiel points in that direction, telling us outright not to blame others for our plight: "It is only the person who sins that shall die" (18:4). People are responsible for their own actions, not anyone else's. No one is compelled to do evil. When we sin, we mimic the transgression of Adam, and our freedom is circumscribed by fallen history. Freedom is never more than finite freedom, and after the Fall it gets circumscribed by the sinful dynamics of history.

Agents are expected to respond to the situation they face and to influence the future as they can. They act within limiting conditions—but they do act. In a crime of murder, for example, there are always mitigating circumstances. There may have been violence in the home; the murderer himself may have been the victim of abuse. But the crime is still taken seriously by the legal system. We never say the murderer *had* to do it and could not help it. In our own thinking we recognize both social and individual responsibility, just as the Bible does.

It is important to add that although we are fallen creatures, we are still bearers of the image of God. We participate in God's image now under the conditions of sin, but the likeness is not annihilated. The ember is still glowing. We can repent and respond to God's call to return like the prodigal. Indeed, God repeatedly calls on us to turn to him and be saved, and this is a genuine invitation. God takes no pleasure in the death of the wicked, but wants them to turn from evil and live (Ezek 33:11).[6]

We may add further that this is true of anyone anywhere. One can relate to the God of heaven and earth on the basis of the image and the presence of the Spirit of God in the whole creation. Sinners may not be able to find God—but God can find them. Christ died for them, and God can apply the benefits of redemption to them as he did with Job. The Hound of Heaven can pursue the sinner until the decision is made to return or remain in isolation. As Peter states, "In every nation anyone who fears [God] and does what is right is acceptable to him" (Acts 10:35).[7]

Forensic Theism and Sin

Forensic theism views sin primarily as infraction and God as a Judge who makes rules and assigns penalties for disobedience. Sin is defined primarily as disobedience to the rules. Islam, like Pharisaism at the time of Jesus, is a religion that satisfies people who want authoritative direction on what is right and wrong. They accept that they are imperfect but want assurance that there are actions that if taken will enable them to make up for any sins they have committed. As noted in an earlier chapter, the requirements of Islam are by no means impossible for ordinary men and women to satisfy: confess the name of God and Muhammad his prophet, pray five times a day, do a few other duties, and you are on your way to heaven.

Sometimes Christians have the same mentality. They think they will be accepted if they do their best, if they give to charity, are kind to animals, help those in trouble and so on. Sin is human imperfection, and since (happily) God does not require perfection, we can attain a passing grade by paying attention to the prescriptions.

Other versions of forensic theism take sin much more seriously than that. They may say that God has decreed only perfection to be acceptable, that there is no passing grade. A single sin would be enough to condemn us, and ignorance is no excuse. Everyone is guilty because of the sin of Adam. His infraction resulted in all humans' being pronounced guilty and destined for hell. Even children are condemned from their first breath. Depravity is so grave that it is thought impossible for sinners to turn to God even though he calls them. God chooses some to be saved and sends the rest off to eternal death.[8]

There is a certain amount of comfort in such a model. Assuming you know that you have been chosen, there is assurance. If you have understood the gospel and accepted it, you are presumed to be born again and among the elect. You can be sure that God has a place for you in the lifeboat.

Unfortunately, the forensic model makes God appear immoral and less loving than human parents generally are with their children. But such objections may be of little concern to forensic theists who assume that God has the perfect right to make the rules as he chooses and who believe that any critical questioning of God's authority is blasphemous. This is how they hear the apostle Paul:

> Who indeed are you, a human being, to argue with God? Will what is molded say to the one who molds it, "Why have you made me like this?" Has the potter no right over the clay, to make out of the same lump one object for special use and another for ordinary use? What if God, desiring to show his wrath and to make known his power, has endured with much patience the objects of wrath that are made for destruction? (Rom 9:20-22)

If every lump of clay is spoiled with original sin, according to this view, God is perfectly just in sending any person to hell. And if we are among the few who are lucky enough to be chosen, we can magnify God's grace without feeling bad about the others who get the hell their sin deserves anyway.

Of course we question that this is what Paul was getting at. The passage about the potter has nothing to do with individual guilt and salvation. These words of Jeremiah refer to God's dealings with the nation of Israel and have no arbitrariness attached to them.

Catholic and Orthodox Understandings

At the Council of Trent, the Counter-Reformation purged crasser elements of ritualism from the Catholic tradition, but agreement concerning original sin remained between Protestants and Catholics. Augustine's theory that all humans deserve damnation from birth was accepted by both sides. What Protestants and Roman Catholics disagreed about was the *remedy* for original sin. Roman Catholic theologians denied the imputed righteousness proclaimed by Protestants and taught that original sin could be reversed by an impartation of grace through baptism and other sacraments of the church.

Neither side seemed much concerned about the moral objection that those outside the narrowly defined "grace" of God were consigned to hell because of original sin. The Augustinian interpretation just fed the need to save the heathen from that fate and fueled the zeal of missionaries like Francis Xavier, who once had water thrown over six thousand fishermen in West India as he recited the baptismal formula and afterward reported to the pope that thousands of souls had been saved.

A similar logic required nurses in hospitals to baptize babies in danger of dying, to save them from hell. Given the model that considers the heart of every newborn to be infected by original sin, the rule was logical enough. Only in the twentieth century have Catholic and Protestant theologians been able to understand things better. A change of theological model has taken place, a softening of the view that original sin condemns all of humanity automatically to hell. With the reforms of Vatican II, a different doctrine has appeared. Sin in modern Catholic doctrine is explained more as a defective heart attitude and broken relationships. It would be hard to find a Catholic theologian nowadays who would consider that the unbaptized and all non-Catholics go to hell.[9]

The Greek Orthodox understanding is that sin reveals humanity's need to become like God again, experiencing what is called deification. Sin has marred the image of God, and the solution is to have one's eyes opened (by sharing in the liturgy) to heavenly and incarnational realities. Orthodox theology never asserted that there was no salvation outside the church but assumed the church was involved in the salvation of the whole human race. The Western theory of original sin never made sense to the Greek fathers, who did not see it in the New Testament and wisely avoided it.

Sin in Creative Love Theism

In creative love theism, sin is a misuse of human freedom and a repudiation of the divine love—a view that looks more to Irenaeus than to Augustine.[10] Sin is not connected to bodily existence or any natural condition. It is a universal condition as well as a freely chosen act for which we are responsible. Sin is more than the corruption of individuals; it is a power active in corporate structures as well as individual lives. We are dealing with an encompassing reign of evil and a solidarity of humanity in sin and alienation from which God wishes to set us free.

The story of Adam eating the forbidden fruit should not be interpreted according to judicial models. The Fall was a disruption of family relationships: persons fell out of loving relationship with God and one another. God wanted to engage in conversation with them, but they hid from him. The loving relationship was broken by our betrayal, with the result that the couple were ashamed and sought to hide rather than continue the conversation with God. Then things went badly wrong between the man and the woman themselves also, and instead of loving they begin to blame one another.

The story is inexhaustible; for example, it has feminist implications. Men and women were created to be social beings in harmony, and both were appointed to exercise dominion over the creation. What went wrong in the Fall was that the man usurped dominion for himself and began to impose it in illegitimate ways at the expense of the woman, while the woman fell into a subordinate role that also corrupted the intended mutual relationship.

How we define sin makes an important difference for how the remedy is understood. Healthy parents, even when betrayed, do not condemn or exclude their children. Their desire is to enjoy reconciliation and for the child to be freed from whatever is preventing participation in loving family relationships. In the same way, God is not obsessed with the guilt of our sins but with the matter of restoration. He longs and works for the liberation of his creatures. Forgiveness is needed, and penitence too, but the bottom line is that God still loves us though we have failed.

Creative love theism works with the picture of two modes of existence. Adam turned in the direction of death, but Abraham looked away from the curse of sin to God who raises the dead (Rom 4:18-22). Anyone with faith is a person moving from the grip of death toward the freedom of a full life. Death in Adam and life in Christ are the alternatives God sets forth before all humans.

Creative love theism frees us from a picture of a God who condemns us for legal infractions. It offers the good news of a loving God who is for all people everywhere.

VI

JUDGMENT
Caring
Love

CREATIVE LOVE THEISM HAS A SPECIAL WAY OF ORDERING THE LOVE AND judgment of God. Love is accompanied by judgment, but not along parallel lines as in the doctrine of double predestination. God's judgment serves God's grace—he says yes to the world, not yes and no (2 Cor 1:20). His love is not ambiguous or doubtful. God judges our sin but in his heart wants to have mercy on us all (Rom 11:32). We think of judgment as God's caring love, over against distorted ideas about wrath held by some. It is wrong to imagine divine wrath as an attribute of God like his mercy, as though God had competing and even conflicting attributes that led him sometimes to forgive and other times to condemn.

Love and Wrath

To correct this misreading of the gospel, it is necessary to clarify the relationship between God's love and God's wrath. Calvinism has tended to regard wrath as a function of divine holiness and to sever its relation to love. This gives the impression of a split in the deity, with one part clamoring for condemnation and the other part yearning to forgive. This leads, then, to a view of redemption in which there is a problem in God that has to be overcome—as if God had to be persuaded to love sinners almost against his nature. It may be theorized that the justice component in God has to be requited by the mercy component to win him over to a policy of reconciliation for humanity.

One thing that can be said for this view is that it takes sin seriously and avoids depicting God's love in a sentimental way. But the idea of a split in God, a problem needing resolution if humanity is to be saved, is intolerable. We cannot believe that there are two gods and two divine wills—one longing to save and the other needing to condemn.

Luther came perilously close to saying so when he spoke of a hidden and a revealed God, of a will that desires to save and a will that secretly decides to reject. This is a dangerous and unhappy dualism. God's wrath in response to sin cannot be divorced from his love for sinners, but is to be seen as an expression of it. As Paul Jewett said, "Wrath describes not God as he is in himself but as he is related to the sinner who spurns his love and dishonors his name."[1]

When we relate love and wrath, it is important to recognize that God's wrath is in the service of his love. Love and wrath are not equally ultimate in the divine nature like two parallel attributes: instead, wrath is subordinate to love. This is clear in many texts; for example,

The LORD, the LORD,
a God merciful and gracious,
slow to anger,
and abounding in steadfast love and faithfulness. (Ex 34:6)

Although there *is* wrath (contrary to liberal theology), God's love but not his wrath is everlasting. If God were wrath in the same way that he is love, God would be internally schizophrenic. The Trinity is a fellowship of love, not of anger. Wrath arises in relation to sinners who spurn divine love. Betrayal calls for a vigorous response; God's wrath arises from injured love. But wrath must not be seen in isolation from concern for humanity.[2]

Wrath is an indicator not of God's dark side (which does not exist—in him is no darkness at all) but of God's response to humanity's treatment of him. God is not indifferent to what we do when we sin, and so wrath arises in him. It is a measure of his concern for us that he is *not* indifferent to us. Concern is the *source* of his anger—it is not its opposite. Paradoxically, if God is angry with us it is because he loves us. What would be truly awful would be if God didn't care, if he were indifferent to our evil and even condoned it.

God's anger is aroused when the rights of the poor are violated, when orphans and widows are oppressed and when his name is blasphemed. But it is aroused because he loves sinners, not because he hates them. If he did not love them, he would let things be as they are and give up. The story of the flood in Genesis suggests that God almost reached that point once but, thankfully, drew back (6:6-8).

Slow to Anger

The Bible stresses the fact that God restrains his anger when it does arise. The Bible says that God is good and is *slow* to anger. God does not like anger in us because he does not even like it in himself. Think of the book of Jonah, which tells how God wants to repent of the evil that he said he would do to Nineveh. He really longs for the Ninevites to repent so that he will not have to judge them. God does not want to be angry, and his wrath only happens when people remain stubbornly impenitent, when they leave God no alternative but to act in judgment. But even then God would much rather do them good, because he is compassionate by nature.

When God's anger does burn against sinners, the Bible says it lasts only a moment. His anger passes, but his love endures forever. Wrath happens, but it does not abide. Because God's anger is rooted in his love for us, it is actually distasteful to him. It is a tragic necessity, not something God ever delights in. It causes him suffering and means he must suspend his mercy for a time.

Paul tells us not to avenge ourselves but to leave wrath to God (Rom 12:19). This may be because we cannot handle it without being vindictive. Compare this with what Isaiah says about God judging Egypt. The prophet says that God is going to make himself known to the Egyptians but will have to come down hard on them first: "The LORD will strike Egypt, striking and healing; they will return to the LORD, and he will listen to their supplications *and heal them*" (Is 19:22).

Our point is that God's wrath is not a fundamental disposition inherent in God's nature but a reaction that God experiences because of his love when he is confronted by sin. Jeremiah knew that God's mercy is greater than his justice:

Although our iniquities testify against us,

act, O LORD, for your name's sake. (Jer 14:7)

Even in judgment, God acts out of love: "I reprove and discipline those whom I love" (Rev 3:19). The principle is plain:

Although [God] causes grief, he will have compassion
   according to the abundance of his steadfast love;
for he does not willingly afflict
   or grieve anyone. (Lam 3:32)

The matter is clear. God is love, and he manifests wrath when spurned. This is what any real lover does. Clearly God's purpose is to save, not to condemn or destroy. "God did not send the Son into the world to condemn the world, but in order that the world might be saved through him" (Jn 3:17). When Jesus encountered the woman taken in adultery, he did not condemn her (Jn 8:11). He just wanted her to change.

God's judgments, when they fall in advance of the final judgment, are intended to lead men and women to repentance (Rom 2:4). Because, as Peter says, "the Lord is . . . not wanting any to perish, but all to come to repentance" (2 Pet 3:9). His threat to remove the lampstand from a church, for example (Rev 2:5), is to provoke conversion. God wants to have mercy on all people, if possible (Rom 11:32).

The purpose of judgment is mercy. If God had his way, all his judgments would be penultimate, and everyone would be saved. Only when judgments fail to provoke repentance do they provoke eschatological wrath. Only when the final no is rendered does God close the books on the impenitent (Rom 2:5). Before that they remain open. (We will return to this point in chapter eight.)

Judgment and Salvation

Let us try now to view God's judgments in the context of his saving purposes. Yes, God judges sinners, but his judgments are those of a lover, not those of an angry judge. God is the Savior of the world, who cares about what is just and right even in his act of saving. The context for viewing God's judgments is not the courtroom but the family. Judgment is the reaction of trinitarian love to sin.

Should there be a final refusal to repent, God's judgments may mean final judgment and irrevocable rejection. The finally impenitent will be swept away in fury—we do not intend to sidestep clear biblical warnings to that effect. But the judgments in history *prior* to final judgment are not meant as God's last word. Judgments upon nations, cities, peoples, churches, families and individuals are meant to warn and deter, heal and restore. They are not proof that God does not love us but proof that he does. Paul states that the judgments that fall on disobedient Israel serve the divine purpose that has for its end God's having mercy upon them all (Rom 11:32).

God is a father who would heal his broken creatures, not a judge thirsty to condemn them. He wants us all, without exception, to turn back from folly and grow into conformity with the image of his Son. His judgments have a loving and constructive purpose. His wrath falls upon men and women in order to warn, correct and teach them. Human actions in a moral universe have consequences and incur judgments, but the judgments fall so that sinners might learn, change and grow. God's wrath does not mean that he hates us.

Not all biblical texts make this as clear as others do. The prophet Nahum, for example, does not seem to see it that way from his brief oracle. Perhaps it was not yet revealed to him. Old Testament writers often display a less than Christian point of view even when they teach some truth. It is possible to cite texts of judgment, such as the account of the destruction of Sodom and Gomorrah, where there does not seem to be any concern to correct and restore sinners but only to destroy them.

But this truth is more often present than acknowledged. Take the book of Revelation. Many read it as a book of terrible judgments that result in the damnation of all but a few persons. But is this the best way to read it? And, by extension, is it the best way to read the Bible as a whole?

The book of Revelation itself alerts us not to interpret in this manner. It tells us that overarching the throne of God is a rainbow (4:3). This is a signal not to interpret the disasters that follow as if God had forgotten his promise to Noah and his covenant with all flesh. The visionary wants us to interpret the coming ordeals described in the book as part of a process that has its goal as the salvation of the nations. God is going to succeed and not fail to bring a chaotic world under his sovereignty. It won't be easy, it won't be painless, but it will be done.

It is wrong to read John as if he were saying that God is going to be happy with saving a mere vestige of fallen humanity and has given up on the world as a whole. On the contrary, John the Divine expects God's purposes to triumph in the new heavens and earth, even though there will be considerable judgment first. There is a rottenness to be purged and a great deal of transforming to be done. But God intends to do this through the Lamb who has broken the seals. John is an optimist, not a pessimist. He believes and predicts that all the nations will come and worship God in the end (15:4).

He predicts that after the battles have subsided, the nations will emerge free of Satan's deception and come under God's reign.

How have we missed this point? The smashing of evil forces in Revelation does not refer to the destruction of most humans (as some read it) but to the defeat of the evil powers and the liberation of humanity from their grip. It is a message of victory over evil. John anticipates the day when all the kings of the earth will bring their glory into the new Jerusalem (21:26). There is scarcely a more eloquent statement of the global purposes of God in the Bible.

George Caird gets it right: "The repeated attacks upon the ungodly world ordered by all the armament of heaven, which occupy so large a part of John's book, are designed not to destroy or to punish, but to penetrate the defences which the world has erected against the rule of God." The whole point of this book is that a presently enslaved humanity will be set free and experience healing. This is what God wants to happen and will make happen.[3]

The Judgment of God

It is important to see that God's righteousness is an integral part of his saving work, not something alien to it. According to the forensic model, righteousness and judgment are something to be afraid of. Yet in the Bible one does not fear God's righteousness but hopes in it. The righteousness of God is not something that stands against us to threaten us but something that will ultimately put right what is wrong with the world. Justification is not only a declaring just but is also a putting right. It transcends the forensic level, being both a gift and a power, both a declaring just and a making righteous. God's righteousness is the power of God moving history to new creation.

Justification is a relational term. It has been a mistake to think of justification just as forensic acquittal or legal fiction. Paul is talking about a new relationship with God. God has put things right between us and welcomes us to his family of sons and daughters. Much more than acquittal, justification is a rectification of our relationship with him.[4]

We celebrate God's righteousness as the hope of salvation and do not fear it. Isaiah has it right:

Shower, O heavens, from above,
   and let the skies rain down righteousness;
let the earth open, that salvation may spring up,

and let it cause righteousness to sprout up also. (Is 45:8)

The *righteousness* of God refers to his saving action. God's righteousness has been revealed together with the power to save humanity (Rom 1:17). Righteousness is synonymous with the saving activity of God and allied with God's mercy, the very opposite of condemnatory judgment. Of course, God's righteousness includes the serious demand that humanity return to the order God has established. But it also has in view making this return a possibility. God's justice will rectify and put things right. It aims at restoration, not condemnation, and therefore is a cause of hope, not of fear. God's righteousness is not primarily forensic—it is not to be viewed as a demanding attribute before which we tremble and which demands penal satisfaction. The righteousness of God is not a barrier to salvation but the source of salvation. God's righteousness brings salvation.

What then does it mean to say God is our Judge? This has nothing to do with an internal struggle in God over whether to save or to reject. *God brings his judgment to bear on sin in the work of triumphing over it.* The Judge is our Savior, one who comes to our rescue and delivers us. God accuses us and exposes sin—but only in order to defeat evil in us.

Biblical writers viewed judgment in the context of salvation, not in opposition to it. It is an aspect of God's desire to liberate us. Judgment has mostly to do with ruling and saving. Remember how God raised up "judges" to deliver Israel. They rendered judgments on behalf of his people, judgments in the service of grace. Even in the case of Egypt and Assyria (as we noted), after God has judged them, he says he will also heal them. After all the judgments are passed, God will declare: "Blessed be Egypt my people, and Assyria the work of my hands, and Israel my heritage" (Is 19:25). God wants his judgments to make way for his mercy and not be the last word.

This is not the kind of judging one finds expressed in Islam or in forensic theism generally. According to the Qur'an, we will all stand before the Judge at the last judgment. He will hold the scales of justice and place our good deeds on one side and our bad deeds on the other. If our good deeds outweigh the bad ones, we will go to heaven. If the Judge decides there is more bad than good, we'll go to hell.

The model that has been dominant in the Western church is more subtle but not altogether dissimilar. The thinking goes like this: Because of original sin all people are consigned to hell. Jesus came into our world and died on the cross as a substitute. He made the payment that was sufficient to be a just penalty for our sins, an atonement that could be credited to our account.

One question has been how the atonement would be credited to our account. Roman Catholics believed it was by baptism and submission to the church under papal authority. Calvinists believed Christ's saving work was credited to those whom God predestined. Nineteenth-century evangelicals believed that those who heard the gospel and responded in repentance and faith could be saved. All others deserved to go to hell, and God as Judge was bound to send them there.

This pattern of thinking pictures God in a law-court setting instead of in a family. In the family model, the love of God is viewed like that of a loving parent encouraging children to become loving. Any judging of such a parent is a part of loving. This is in contrast to the judicial model, where wrath flows against sinners in a courtroom setting as people are condemned before an awesome judge. In that picture God starts loving only when his justice has been satisfied. Is there any doubt which picture fits biblical revelation?

God the Judge

The biblical picture is one of hope. God wants to bless all the families of earth in Abraham. The expectation is for all the nations to come before God and worship him. But before that will happen, we get to hear about judgment. God is driven to judgment because there is so much garbage to clear away before this future can be realized. The goal is steady though the road may be rocky—God wants the salvation of his creatures and does not give up on them (Hosea 11:8-9). He is faithful to his promises, come what may, even if it means doing new things to open up the future, that his grace may be realized.

Jesus is in line with this. He proclaims his mission to be the inception of the kingdom of God, but not yet in fullness. Many judgments will have to fall before its consummation. Still, God's desire is not judgment but salvation.

Maybe in order to grasp the meaning of judge and judgment, we need to take a fresh look at the book of Judges, because it tells us how the Jewish people saw judges functioning. Judges were leaders empowered by the Holy Spirit to set people free from oppression. Deborah, Gideon and Samson were not law-court judges—they were leaders who took risks in order to care for people. They fought for the people, they led them out of bondage, and they brought peace. A judge would settle petty quarrels between individuals, while the ordinary business of civil and criminal law was carried on by town elders at the city gate.

In creative love theism, we are trying to picture God as a judge along these lines. God is the kind of judge who is concerned for the liberation of people. He is the Lord who visits and redeems his people from slavery, as in the events of the exodus.

The Jews looked back to King David in this way too. Like the judges, he led the nation against oppressors. He established peace, dealt with quarrels and provided for worship. He was gentle like a shepherd, caring and approachable like a father. It was this kind of judge whom the Jews anticipated in the Servant Messiah. They did not have the picture of a Roman judge.

In the Psalms too, God is appealed to as a Judge who saves and protects his people. God's judgment is not something a conscience-stricken believer has to fear so much as something the believer can hope for. God's kind of healing judgment included the dimension of social justice. Isaiah told the people to "seek justice, rescue the oppressed, defend the orphan, plead for the widow" (see Is 1:11-17). Similarly, in Hosea God says: "I desire steadfast love and not sacrifice" (Hosea 6:6). Micah asks rhetorically, "What does the LORD require of you but to do justice, and to love kindness, and to walk humbly with your God?" (Micah 6:8). Justice was not a law-court category but a word of salvation, including an active concern for the needy.

In the Old Testament, God is the Judge of nations and individuals after the manner of the leaders in Judges, like the just and caring ruler pictured in Psalms and like a loving parent assigning consequences for the good of the children. His aim is not to exclude but to restore. When parents get angry and assign consequences that seem unfair, children need reassurance that they are still loved. For the same reason, reassurances of the love of God are often given in the Scriptures. Believing that God still loves us even when bad consequences descend on us is an important component of faith.

How does the New Testament see God's judging? The central point may be found in Jesus' message. Unlike Jews of his day, who would have limited salvation to Israel, he promised a share in it to the Gentiles. Regarding a Jewish town that did not welcome the disciples, Jesus says, "Truly I tell you, it will be more tolerable for the land of Sodom and Gomorrah on the day of judgment than for that town" (Mt 10:15). Whereas Rabbi Hyrcanus denied that the people of Sodom would be raised, Jesus said they would be. The Queen of Sheba, the men and women of Nineveh and even the wicked sinners of Sodom will arise in the resurrection; all the nations without exception will stand before God, according to Jesus. Their appearance may be to confirm that the judgments they suffered in history were final, or it may be to show to them some unexpected mercy. Just because Sodom was destroyed in early times, it does not follow that it has no hope at the end of history. To many who do not expect it Jesus will say, "Come, you that are blessed by my Father" (see Mt 25:31-46).

Jesus did not view Israel as a vessel of mercy while all Gentiles would go to perdition. In the last judgment, any distinction between Jew and Gentile is to disappear, and God will show mercy to all people. From the east and the west, from north and south, they will come to sit at table with Abraham in the kingdom of God (Mt 8:11). The same justice will be measured out to Gentiles as to Jews. The glory of the Lord will be revealed to the whole world, and the Gentiles will come to God's mountain to worship. They too will belong to the people of God and will partake in the messianic banquet.

As Isaiah said:

On this mountain the LORD of hosts will make for all peoples

a feast of rich food, a feast of well-aged wines,

of rich food filled with marrow, of well-aged wines strained clear.

And he will destroy on this mountain

the shroud that is cast over all peoples,

the sheet that is spread over all nations;

he will swallow up death forever.

Then the Lord GOD will wipe away the tears from all faces,

and the disgrace of his people he will take away from all the earth.

(Is 25:6-8)

Although the Old Testament speaks much about the judgment of the nations, Jesus sees them as eventually incorporated into the kingdom of God.

Jesus' hearers in Matthew 10 and Luke 10 would have known about the destruction of Sodom and Gomorrah in Abraham's day. They would have known about the devastation of the cities of Tyre and Sidon a few hundred years before their day by the armies of Alexander. Jesus is warning them that cities in Galilee could be similarly ravaged in that generation if they did not repent. Even today countries are ravaged by civil war and invading armies. They are prey to terrible disasters and upheavals. Sometimes prophets are able to give reasons for the disaster—sometimes not, as in the case of Job, where no apparent cause for the disasters he suffered can be discerned. In such a case, we must believe that God is just even though the explanation is not available.

In creative love theism, God certainly does judge nations and individuals, but his judging has the character of mercy. God is like an Old Testament judge, a just and caring king, a loving parent who assigns consequences to actions. God cares, protects, defends, frees, intervenes, fights for, sends into exile, brings back from exile, but all the while keeps on loving us and wants never to exclude anyone, even though some may exclude themselves.

VII

ADVENT
Active
Love

T HE COMING OF JESUS CHRIST IN POWER AND GLORY IS VITAL TO THE BIBLICAL message. We call it advent, and it is so central that a theology could be written with hope as its integrating theme.[1] We await what Paul calls the "blessed hope and the manifestation of the glory of our great God and Savior, Jesus Christ" (Tit 2:13). The resurrection inaugurated the age of salvation anticipated by the Old Testament, and the risen Lord has poured out the Spirit of life to restore the creation. One day the kingdom of God will be consummated, and the creation will be liberated from bondage to corruption (Rom 8:21). When the kingdom comes, evil will be overcome and the goal of creation realized. More than the survival of disembodied souls, it will be a redemption both personal and communal, involving spirit and body, affecting church and cosmos. Our hope for fulfillment is also deeply relevant in a day when many people are living aimlessly and without hope.[2]

What Is Advent?
The meaning of *advent* is basically simple. Not a puzzle to be figured out by the makers of prophecy charts, it is faith's confidence that Jesus is coming, that the new order he proclaimed will be realized and that what he stood for

will prove solid and reliable. Hope is the response to the future of those who believe the good news, who are confident in the fulfillment of God's promises. It is not a question of predicting the date or imagining what the new creation will be like. We cannot know that any more than the unborn can know the date of their birth or what life outside the womb will be like. Hope does not mean information about times and seasons; it is confidence in the coming victory of God. This hope empowers us to live as disciples.

God calls us to be witnesses to the kingdom, and hope strengthens our resolve to persist in obedient action. We are called to be active participants in the mending of creation with Jesus, and hope enables us to live not for ourselves but for him who died and rose again. It gives us courage and fortitude to stand with Jesus, to live in solidarity with those who suffer and to act like disciples who await the kingdom of God.

Why is the meaning of advent often distorted by people who set dates and create false expectations? One would think that repeated failures to set the date correctly would put a stop to this practice.

The explanation is in part innocent. The Bible is not an easy book to read and understand, especially in this area, and it can be misunderstood when one takes a naive approach. There are passages like Daniel 9:24-27 and Revelation 12:6 that do appear to offer a chronology of future events, even though a closer reading suggests they do not. A modern reader may fail to understand the symbolism important to an ancient writer. It may require biblical specialists to sort out the difficult texts in this area.

At the same time, ordinary readers can see that the Bible speaks of advent in picture language and warns us against attempting to calculate dates (Acts 1:6-7). One can readily grasp the wisdom of God in not making the date of the Second Coming known. Keeping it a secret (or not fixing it rigidly) makes good sense, since it leaves God free to act when and how he chooses. It also prevents us from taking a fatalistic attitude, which results when we know too much about the timetable of events. If the advent were to happen tomorrow, for example, it would be better not to know it today, because it would prevent us from doing this day's duty.

The Nature of Biblical Prophecy

Biblical prophecies are often conditional. They announce possibilities so as to give people an opportunity to change the future. For example, God actually did not want the prophecy he gave to Jonah against the city of

Nineveh to happen. God hoped that if this prophetic warning was given, the judgment might be avoided. History is not programmed but involves human choices. Prophets speak of hope and judgment in order to influence our actions. They leave room for God to fulfill their oracles in ways that transcend the original terms.

Who from reading the Old Testament could have predicted exactly what Jesus would be like? Who could have predicted exactly what would happen? There was much newness and surprise in the fulfillment of the promises. God gave more than he had promised to. Jesus' enemies were biblical literalists who balked at Jesus precisely because he did not fit their expectation of what Messiah would be like—a picture carefully constructed from the Bible. In Christ's coming, God exercised creativity that did not meet their expectations and went beyond what had been anticipated.

As a general rule, one should approach biblical statements about the coming kingdom as one would approach the assertions about creation. Both deal with things no eye has seen or can see. In both cases language is stretched to the limit.[3] A more intelligent reading of the Bible is one way to avoid distorting the biblical hope.

Preparation for the Coming

There can be a darker aspect of the problem of misunderstanding than hermeneutics. In their zeal to calculate the date of the advent, people may be subconsciously wanting to avoid facing up to the real thrust of Christian hope, which is to impact the lives of disciples. Calculation can easily eclipse that. The advent or coming of Christ is meant to spur us to costly discipleship consistent with the kingdom that is coming. We are told to be like the maidens in the parable who, because they expected the bridegroom's coming, made themselves ready for it. Those who spend their time calculating the date of the end times are in danger of being like the foolish maidens, who were so intrigued by speculation about the time of the bridegroom's arrival that they failed to get ready for it (Mt 25:1-13). There is a real danger of getting sidetracked.

Amos had to say to some in his day: "Alas for you who desire the day of the LORD! Why do you want the day of the LORD? It is darkness, not light" (Amos 5:18). His point was that the key thing is not to be experts in prophecy but to be engaged in the kind of obedient action that would testify to the coming kingdom. So the foolish maidens in Jesus' parable symbolize believers who think they have a handle on the time of the advent but do not concentrate on letting their light shine.

Mini-Advents

We anticipate a final advent, but there are also mini-advents. They are less talked about. By *mini-advents* we mean acts of God in history which anticipate and advance the kingdom of God.

There is a final judgment, and there are mini-judgments in advance of it, judgments in history that anticipate the final event. There are penultimate judgments such as Israel's exile into Babylon, the fall of Jerusalem and the outworking of the consequences of sin in people's lives prior to the last judgment. They serve as warnings meant to lead to repentance. Not to respond to them, as Paul says, is to store up wrath on that last day (Rom 2:4-5).

The Bible speaks in the same way about the advent or coming of Christ. There are also comings in history prior to it. The advent is anticipated by mini-comings, some not so minor. Jesus comes not only on the last day but throughout the history of the world. He indicates this when he says to the church of Ephesus that needed to repent, "Repent, and do the works you did at first. If not, *I will come to you* and remove your lampstand from its place" (Rev 2:5). Christ is not inactive, sitting at God's right hand. He is working through the Spirit to set us free, and coming to us is one of his ways of dealing with the effects of human sin and freeing people before it is too late.

The "little apocalypse" of Mark 13 is a fascinating chapter, and it can illustrate our point.[4] When you read it, it sounds as if Jesus is predicting that the world is about to end. This led Albert Schweitzer to claim that Jesus made an error in announcing a kingdom that failed to materialize. He claimed that Jesus predicted the end of the world and it did not happen. Jerusalem was destroyed, all right, but the Son of Man did not return and the judgment did not fall. As a result, Jesus died a failure.

But isn't it more likely that Mark 13 is referring to events in the first century, not at the end of the world? We believe that Jesus is referring to a coming, but not to the Second Coming. He is speaking of a coming in advance of advent, an event that was to happen in the first century and that would mark the end of an era and the passing of a generation.

As for the final advent, it will occur at the end of history, but we are not told when that will happen. Of the last advent Jesus says quite plainly: "But about that day or hour no one knows, neither the angels in heaven, nor the Son, but only the Father" (Mk 13:32).

It is likely that in Mark 13 Jesus is speaking of the fall of Jerusalem in apocalyptic terms, warning his hearers that they are about to experience a coming or mini-advent of God in history. The language sounds a little extravagant to us, but it is consistent with the way prophets spoke about turning points in world history. It is even the way we ourselves sometime speak when alluding to an "earth-shattering" event like the fall of communism. We do not mean the words literally. The earth was not really shattered. This is metaphorical language for another serious matter. Such events are indeed more important than earth tremors, because they change the course of history itself.

Apocalyptic language tells us that history is to experience a major turn-around, that a day of liberation is at hand. God's kingdom is drawing near—one era is coming to an end, another is beginning. We must not think of Jesus as if he were a literalist, as if he did not know that cloud imagery, for example, concerned more than water vapor. With his imagery Jesus was referring to space-time events that were about to happen to the inhabitants of Palestine, and he used prophetic language to underline their enormous significance. Judgment was about to fall upon Israel, but it was not the final judgment. Christ was about to come, but not in the last advent.[5]

Jesus' talk about stars falling from heaven and the sun being darkened is end-of-the-world language to describe an important event that was about to happen. The imagery came from Isaiah's words about the fall of Babylon (chap. 13), which was metaphorical for the fall of a city long ago. Other prophets used similar metaphors (for example, Ezek 32:7-8; Joel 2:1-10, 30-31). They were thinking not of physical portents in the sky but of catastrophic events in history.

Jesus' warnings about the future did not refer to the end of the world but to judgments about to fall in time-space. Citing Isaiah's oracle about the fall of Babylon, he was picturing the eclipse of a great nation: just as Babylon suddenly fell to the ground, so it would be with Jerusalem.

Actual history supports our interpretation. The world did not come to an end in A.D. 70 with the destruction of Jerusalem. The facts now fit the exegetical argument we have offered. Jesus was certainly speaking of an advent prior to the final day of the Lord. Thus an advent or parousia took place at the close of the Old Testament dispensation. It was a local event in

Judea in the first century, witnessed by the generation then living, and the language used to describe it was stock-in-trade prophetic language in which present judgments anticipate the final judgment.

This application is visible in other biblical texts. "When the tenants saw the [owner's] son, they said to themselves, 'This is the heir; come, let us kill him.' . . . Now when the owner of the vineyard comes, what will he do to those tenants? . . . He will put those wretches to a miserable death, and lease the vineyard to other tenants" (Mt 21:38-41). The judgment here is a historical judgment on Jesus' tormentors, as in Matthew 22:7. The Roman legions were going to march on Jerusalem and to destroy it, and in their attack a divine judgment would be felt. This reminds us of the Old Testament, where God uses Cyrus and the Assyrians to do his work.

The Day of the Lord

There is a last advent, and there are mini-advents before it. There are many comings and visitations, because God is a God of action. Idols cannot do anything, says Isaiah, but the Lord is powerful to save (Is 46). He is the living God, and history is the sphere of his activity. Moses asks:

Has any god ever attempted to go and take a nation for himself from the midst of another nation, by trials, by signs and wonders, by war, by a mighty hand and an outstretched arm, and by terrifying displays of power, as the LORD your God did for you in Egypt before your very eyes? To you it was shown so that you would acknowledge that the LORD is God; there is no other besides him. (Deut 4:34-35)

God makes himself known by acts and judgments in history. This is how God is known—not through speculative thinking, but by what God does in history.

In the Old Testament God came to Adam and Eve in the Garden, and he came again at the destruction of the Tower of Babel. He came to Sarah to give her a child and visited the Israelites in Egypt to bring them into the Promised Land. His coming may destroy the old order, as in the fall of Samaria and the northern kingdom, as in the first fall of Jerusalem and the Babylonian captivity. Or he may come to bless and liberate. There are many comings and visitations of the Lord.

The expression "day of the LORD" occurs dozens of times in the Old Testament. The prophets used it for a momentous event like the exodus. It was a day of the Lord when a nation of slaves was freed to go to the Promised

Land and when divine judgment fell on Egypt. Centuries later, the fall of
Jerusalem to the Babylonians was a victory for Nebuchadnezzar but a day of
catastrophe and exile for the children of Israel.

The expression comes again and again. It refers to the fall of Babylon (Is
13:9), to victory over the armies of Egypt (Jer 46:10), to the fall of Jerusalem
(Ezek 13:5) and to the doom of nations (Ezek 30:3). It points to a day when
God intervenes to judge or bless, to a time when God's mighty hand is evident
in history.

The idea of God's visitations in history occurs in the New Testament as
well. Zechariah, father of John the Baptist, declared: "Praise be to the Lord,
the God of Israel, because he has come and has redeemed his people" (Lk
1:68 NIV). In the incarnation God came to dwell with us. James said in an
address to the Jerusalem church, "Simeon has related how God first looked
favorably on the Gentiles, to take from among them a people for his name"
(Acts 15:14).

God's visitations have different purposes. It may be to encourage a person,
family, church or nation in time of distress. It may be to judge and destroy,
as in Mark 13, where Jesus warns that the Lord will come to destroy the
temple and the city. The fall of Jerusalem was a day of God that brought
judgment on the nation for its hardness of heart. On the other hand, it was
also a day when a worldwide mission would begin and the Gentiles would
start to be gathered in.

We may speak of a day of the Lord in relation to the fall of Rome or
Constantinople, to the French or American revolution, to the toppling of
the Third Reich or to the end of communism. These events were earth-shak-
ing and happened in the context of the providence of God. If we had eyes
to see it, the sign of the Son of Man would be evident in all of them. The
final advent will terminate history, but only when what has to be done
beforehand is done.

Day of Liberation

We can see God's coming in the liberation of peoples. In 1989 there was a
great liberation from the oppressive hand of Marxism. Countries awoke to
unexpected freedom with little shedding of blood. This liberation had roots
in the churches, where many who were concerned about freedom and justice
had continued to pray, keeping the dream of freedom alive. Their hope for
the kingdom of God spelled a defeat of evil and a triumph of good.

Communism was exposed as a false millennialism that had sought salvation by political means. It had led to the death of an estimated 100 million people. Yet it was not brought down by diplomacy or the force of arms; its defeat came through a triumph of the human spirit, which relativized the political and kept the future open for God's kingdom. It did not happen because the church played a clever political game, but as a result of the church's being a light in the darkness. Liberation came because the church preached the risen Lord. Jesus can be seen in the revolution of 1989, and we expect more from his hand in history before we arrive at the new Jerusalem.[6]

This is but one of many movements of liberation that have occurred thanks to God's grace. The United States began with a cry for liberation from foreign control. Then came the concern for the liberation of slaves and eventually full civil rights for black people. Similar concerns surfaced in the struggle against apartheid in South Africa. Liberation theology has focused on the poor in South America, and now other oppressed minorities have begun to see opportunities. The need for women to exercise their gifts in church and society is being addressed with much creative thinking.

These movements are not political accidents. They are rooted in the actions of God and the work of the Spirit. God has created us to love and be loved, and he is burdened by every interference with the freedom to love caused by the system of sin that grips us. Our risen Lord continually comes to us and intervenes on our behalf to free our world from every kind of oppression.

One form of oppression from which people need to be delivered is religious oppression. Such liberation also happens in history in advance of the advent. Idols are shown to be mute and powerless. History is the graveyard of false gods: Baal, Astarte, Zeus and Rimmon—all gone and forgotten, while the Lord lives in the lives of unnumbered millions today. Jesus Christ has already won significant victories over the powers of darkness in history.

There is a victory needed now in the context of Islam. Our prayer is that God will work in such a way that Islam will open up to Jesus. We do not know exactly what God will do. He may decide to leave Islam alone and allow its attitudes to harden even more. Islam may become even more hostile in the future, or it may soften, as is happening in Indonesia. We do not know what God will do in the short term in such matters. But victories are possible, and we pray for them.

Ultimately we are waiting for the kingdom of God. In the meantime there will be ups and downs, progress and regress, success and failure, advance and setback, ironies and surprises, cross and resurrection. We are not privy to God's strategies prior to the end—we simply wait for a revelation of sovereignty at the end of time. God is extending his rule in history. It is his will that all nations participate in the renewal of creation. God works ceaselessly toward that end, entering into conflict with the powers of darkness and into contest with other gods.

God continually comes to us by the Spirit. Called "the Lord, the giver of life" by the Nicene Creed, the Spirit of God sustains all things. The Spirit hovers over the waters and gives life to every creature; in the Spirit we live and move and have being. In the brokenness of the world, the Spirit renews and empowers life and gives hope (Ps 104:30). More than that, the Spirit draws all people to God.

God has never left himself without witness, and the Spirit never fails to orient humankind to the mystery of life and the coming blessings of God. God is coming to us, wooing and warning us, not only at the end of time, but always.

VIII

HELL
Rejecting
Love

Does creative love theism assume the salvation of everyone? It certainly assumes that God wants that, seeing how he reconciled the whole world and included everyone in his salvation plan (2 Cor 5:18). Since Christ died for *all* the ungodly, God's acceptance of everybody might be thought to be assured: there are no sinners for whom Christ did not atone. The implication of universal salvation is strengthened when the idea is added that God's judgment serves his love. How could there be a final judgment like hell which (presumably) could not serve a redemptive purpose?

Universalism takes seriously God's salvific will and assumes that God will save everyone, if he wants to do so. He could achieve this either by means of sovereign power (overcoming their resistance) or by way of sheer persistence (wearing them down). One way or another, God could see to it that every soul finds its way home. It is suggested that a doctrine of hell is unnecessary in Christianity.[1]

We agree that the salvation of everybody is something God wants and something we want too. But there's a problem. Why are there so many warnings about hell in the Bible if it's not real? Why would Jesus warn against the dread possibility of final rejection (Mt 13:41)? It does appear that some may finally reject God's love and be separated from him forever. The warnings about eternal destruction are clear enough to prevent us from entertaining the hope of universal salvation. Evidently God values human freedom so much that he allows people to reject him finally.

Hell and Human Freedom

The big question surrounding hell, then, is not whether it exists but what its nature is. What kind of hell would cohere with creative love thinking? The nature of hell must not contradict what we know about God's love or require a nonsensical element in our thinking about God. We have to ponder what hell is, if it exists.

Augustine conceived of hell as a literal lake of fire where the damned are embodied in order to burn everlastingly in the flames. This cannot be true, because it contradicts our moral sense and God's moral nature. The idea that a fully conscious creature would undergo physical and mental torture through endless time is plainly sadistic and therefore incompatible with a God who loves humanity. We need an alternative model of hell that could be based on the Bible but not involve such horror.[2]

First, hell cannot be viewed as a vindictive, retributive punishment. Since Jesus bore the sins of the world, we know that God is not in the business of punishing people. Jesus died so that he would not have to do that. Therefore, hell has to be more a matter of self-destruction, the logical result of final rejection of God. God does not choose hell for people—they choose it. God loves the ungodly, even those who reject him finally. He does not choose to break relations with them, though they may have broken relations with him. Hell is a possibility that arises from the human side, out of rebellion and obduracy. It exists for sinners who, though forgiven, steadfastly reject their acceptance by God. God invited them to his supper, but they declined the invitation.

There comes a point when God, who has done everything to bring sinners back into fellowship, gives up trying. God accepts defeat at this point and says, in effect, "Their disposition and direction appear to be fixed. They are a lost cause." To repeat, people are in hell because they choose it—none are sent there against their will. Hell is not retributive punishment.

Hell exists only because humans are free to spurn God's love and can choose to be separate. Freedom entails the possibility of rejection. If love is an offer, it can be accepted or rejected, because it cannot be forced. Hell exists because love can be refused. People can decide to live without God both in this life and forever. We might say it is their entitlement. If in the end they say no to God, then even God cannot save them. If they do not say "Your will be done" to God, they will hear God say "Your will be done" to them. Universal salvation is implausible chiefly because God takes no for an answer.[3]

Not that we should suppose God accepts refusal easily. He does not want us to refuse him and will do a great deal to prevent our doing so. When we consider Christ on the cross, we begin to understand how deep is God's desire not to accept rejection from any person. So it is our decision, not God's, that keeps hell open, because "The Lord is . . . not wanting any to perish, but all to come to repentance" (2 Pet 3:9).

We are not suggesting that it is easy for a person to go to hell—only that it can be done. God's love is offered to all, and hell is not a contradiction of that. Hell exists because love can be rejected. God would like to prevent it but cannot. Yes, there are things God cannot do, and this is one.

Granted, it is a problem understanding why anyone would be so foolish as to refuse God's love. What rationale could there possibly be for such a choice? Perhaps this is what Paul meant when he spoke of the mystery of iniquity (2 Thess 2:7). Why would a person finally reject the love of God? We can see reasons in this life, based upon not knowing how foolish such rejection is—but why would anyone reject God in the end? There can be no act of greater folly. Perhaps Milton was right when he said that Satan prefers to reign in hell than serve in heaven. It seems that there are some who are determined not to love God, though it seems incomprehensible.

Jesus tells us that the criterion of judgment is not verbal profession alone. On the one hand, he says, "Not everyone who says to me, 'Lord, Lord,' will enter the kingdom of heaven, but only the one who does the will of my Father in heaven" (Mt 7:21). On the other hand, he says God welcomes those who did not know they had responded but had in fact done so in acts of love toward the needy (Mt 25:31-46). The criterion is words spoken together with lives lived. The question is whether we have shown mercy to the poor out of an appreciation of God's love. The criterion is not so much orthodox belief as a trust in God's grace which takes the form of love in the service of others.

What Is Hell Like?
Creative love theism does have a doctrine of hell, but hell cannot be an

everlasting vindictive torment. God is not vindictive and does not practice sadism. The lurid portrayals of hellfire in the Christian tradition contradict God's identity, according to the gospel. God is not a pitiless, vengeful judge but One who loves his enemies and dies for them.

The view of hell as everlasting torment in body and soul has been a dark aspect of traditional theology for a long time. The problem has often been compounded by other beliefs such as double predestination—that the damned were not elected to salvation and had no opportunity to escape their fate. Not many Christians find this view tolerable, because there is so little love or justice in it. It makes the defense of our faith practically impossible.[4]

How then might we construe the nature of hell in a way that might be viable? One way would be to interpret the traditional view of hell metaphorically, not literally. This is what C. S. Lewis attempted.[5] Here hell is interpreted as the state of being separated from God, bound up with the decision to reject trinitarian fellowship. Hell thus fulfills the earthly decision to live apart from God and in disregard of others, the decision to reject the call of God and to live for oneself. Under this scenario, hell gives people the opportunity to live boring, self-centered lives forever, if they want to. Hell is not everlasting punishment so much as the appropriate end to a direction chosen. Hell is the proper way to end a life of resistance to God's love. It symbolizes the fact that the goal of life can be missed, that human choices matter and that repentance is required for salvation. A life of self-glory and lovelessness leads to hell and is fulfilled there.

This view is plausible and intelligent. It has the advantage of not having to confront the tradition about hell more directly, though it bends it in a metaphorical direction. Hell is reinterpreted as a place where self-centered lives go on forever. The fire is an image and the pain is mental; as a result, it does not have the same feeling of sadism to it, though its unendingness is frightening. Hell is a version of everlasting Chinese water torture—drip, drip, drip forever.

One problem with this view is that it sounds like an evasion of the biblical witness. How could one say that God destroys body and soul under this scenario? Metaphorical hell is not pleasant, but is it really hell? The picture of hell in Lewis may be drab and dull, but it is no lake of fire. Does it do justice to the terrible imagery in Scripture? And does it avoid the impression that hell involves endless vindictive punishment with no point to it?

There is a second view that we prefer. Though no one can be absolutely certain about the nature of hell, this view seems more credible for several reasons. It is called conditional immortality or annihilationism, and it is gaining ground.[6] The view takes Paul literally when he says the wages of sin is death (Rom 6:23). The idea is that humans were made mortal, with everlasting life being a gift, not a natural capacity. This means that the biblical images of destruction and ruin can be taken to mean the termination of existence—final and irreversible death. The fires of hell, then, do not torture but rather consume the wicked.[7]

E. G. Selwyn comments: "There is little in the New Testament to suggest a state of everlasting punishment, but much to indicate an ultimate destruction or dissolution of those who cannot enter into life: conditional immortality seems to be the doctrine most consonant with the teaching of Scripture."[8]

Of course the Bible is reserved in giving us information about the nature of life after death. Yet when it uses the language of death and destruction to refer to hell, it leaves the distinct impression that hell is closure. The Old Testament sets the stage for the New Testament position in speaking of the wicked fading like grass and being cut off forever (as in Ps 37). It speaks of the wicked being burned up and being no more (Mal 4:1-2). This language fits closely with Jesus' warning that God will destroy body and soul in hell. The apostles use the same imagery of destruction, as when Paul speaks of everlasting destruction falling on the impenitent (2 Thess 1:9). He also says the wicked will reap corruption (Gal 6:8) and God will ultimately destroy them (Phil 1:28). He designates the wages of sin as death and the destiny of the wicked as destruction (Phil 3:19). A fair-minded person might just conclude from these texts that the Bible teaches the destruction of the impenitent.

The Old Testament does not have a doctrine of hell as such. It speaks of people going to Sheol when they die, but this is not hell. The term *hell* used in the Gospels is a Hebrew loanword, *gehenna*, which meant the Valley of Hinnom, an area below the east wall of Jerusalem where rubbish was thrown. It makes sense that the rubbish would be burning with cinders dumped from hearths and the fire smoking endlessly with foul fumes. A mass of rotting flesh and vegetables would be alive with maggots, which Mark captures in a quote from Isaiah: "Their worm never dies, and the fire is never quenched" (Mk 9:48; see Is 66:24). The horror of the scene is palpable.

Not only is this view true to a literal reading of Scripture, but it also is consistent with the nature of God's wrath as discussed in chapter six. We argued that God's anger comes in order to heal sinners, not to visit endless torment on them. If it fails to heal them, hell must be termination, because otherwise the picture would be one of God endlessly tormenting people for no reason except retribution.

Immortality and Justice

Why has the annihilationist possibility not been noticed much before? Why would anybody have turned the notion of destruction into everlasting life in hell, creating this monstrous problem? We attribute it to the influence on theology of the Greek idea of the immortality of the soul. With that view entering the picture, the shift is logical and inevitable. If souls are immortal and hell exists, it follows that the wicked will have to suffer consciously forever in it. If the soul is naturally immortal, it has to spend eternity somewhere. If there is a gehenna of fire, hell has to be a condition of torment. The conclusion flows inexorably from the Greek premise. Thus the word *destruction* gets turned into "everlasting torment."

But the belief in the immortality of the soul is not a biblical view. The Bible points to a resurrection of the whole person as a gift of God, not a natural possession. Humans were not created with a natural capacity for everlasting life—Jesus Christ brought immortality to light through the gospel (2 Tim 1:10) The soul is not an immortal substance that has to exist eternally. Let us just accept exactly what Jesus says: God is able to destroy both body and soul in hell (Mt 10:28). The idea of natural immortality seems to have skewed the Christian teaching about hell. It was a mistake and we should correct it.

Not only is conditional immortality more biblical than a view of hell as everlasting conscious punishment, but it has other advantages as well. First, it does not impute to God the sadistic behavior of torturing people endlessly. God as revealed in Christ is merciful and does not torture people—period. How could one respect, let alone worship, a torturing God? John Stott rightly admits: "I find the concept intolerable and do not understand how people can live with it without either cauterizing their feelings or cracking under the strain."[9]

Our view of hell has to pass the moral test, and the view we are advancing here does so. It does not involve everlasting torture; it does not have anything to do with double predestination. God is justified in destroying the wicked because he respects human choices. Affirming hell means accepting human significance. Sinners are not compelled to love God. They have the moral right to closure. They can choose that, if they want to. In the end God allows us to do and be what we want.

Second, hell as destruction is more just. No set of human choices can deserve everlasting conscious torment. No crime could deserve such punishment. It goes far beyond the Old Testament standard of an eye for an eye and a tooth for a tooth, the standard of strict equivalence. What, we ask, would a sinner have to do to earn everlasting punishment? Even Hitler could not impose everlasting punishment on his victims, horrible though their fate was. Therefore Hitler himself did not deserve everlasting conscious punishment on an eye-for-an-eye basis. This is apart from the fact that Jesus calls us to a higher standard than strict equivalence.

In terms of justice, the traditional view of hell is simply unacceptable. It is a punishment in excess of anything that sinners deserve. It creates a disproportion between sins committed in time and suffering experienced forever.

Besides, no purpose is served by the unending torture of the wicked except vengeance. From Scripture we know that God does not delight in punishment for its own sake. Even the plagues of Egypt were intended to be redemptive for those who would respond to the warning. Unending torment is pointless, wasted suffering that can never produce anything good. Conditional immortality makes better sense in terms of justice. If people refuse God's friendship, it would not be right to visit on them everlasting torment, but it would be right to let them go out of existence as the biblical language implies.

Third, conditional immortality paints a better picture metaphysically. The traditional view leaves things split and divided. It has heaven and hell existing alongside each other forever and history ending badly in a stark dualism. Instead of a victory, rebellion goes on forever in hell under conditions of torment. The new creation is flawed from day one, since evil, suffering and death continue to be real. In the new order, then, there would still be two kingdoms—one belonging to God and one to Satan. This cannot be. Surely in the end God will be completely victorious over sin and death, suffering and Satan. Only if all of them go up in smoke does history end in the unqualified victory of God.

According to the traditional view, darkness will hang over the creation forever. It makes better sense metaphysically to think of hell as final destruction and the dwindling out of existence of the impenitent wicked than to posit the eternal existence alongside God of a disloyal opposition in an unredeemed corner of the new creation. What sort of a new creation would that be?

The traditional view of the nature of hell (that the wicked suffer unending conscious torment) is unbiblical. It was possibly fostered by a Hellenistic view of the soul, it casts a negative light on the character of God, and it is supported by bad arguments. A better case can be made for a view of hell in terms of conditional immortality.

The Destiny of the Unevangelized

Under either view, hell is a grim reality. Even if it is not a torture chamber, hell is serious business. To enter hell is to be rejected by God, to miss the purpose for which one was created and to pass into oblivion while others enter into bliss. Hell is a terrifying possibility: the possibility of using freedom to destroy ourselves.

What about those who die in ignorance of Christ? When do they decide for or against God? When is their destiny settled? The fact that God loves them rules out the possibility that they simply have no chance to be saved. Since Christ died for them, we cannot possibly say that it is just unfortunate that they never learned about it. Obviously God will not give up until those people make a decision about this gift which has their name on it.

There are two real possibilities now being debated among evangelicals. One is the view that the unevangelized can be saved exactly as Job was in the Old Testament. He believed in God on the basis of what had been shown to him and was saved by faith just as any Christian is. Faith pleases God when exercised by a pagan like Melchizedek, a Jew like David or a Christian like Peter (Heb 11:6). The level of theological content is not the decisive issue.[10]

The other possibility is postmortem salvation. Just as babies dying in infancy are saved after death, so the unevangelized can be saved in the hereafter. There are texts in the New Testament that hint at such an outcome (1 Pet 3:18-20; 4:6), and it was commonly believed among the early church fathers.[11]

One can combine these two views and say that decisions in this life set the soul's direction in relation to God, and fuller revelation after death enables the person to pick up where things left off and decide once and for all whether to journey toward or away from God.

We have concluded that the most basic hindrance that keeps people from salvation is a turning away from the love of God, not an infraction of the rules. Despite our acts of betrayal, God persists in coming graciously to us. Even his wrath is intended to bring about our conversion and reconciliation. If we refuse, if the final decision is against God's grace, even hell is not vengeful or retributive but a decision to terminate life since nothing positive remains for it.

PART THREE
Doctrine
of
Salvation

DOCTRINES OF SALVATION FOCUS ON THE DIVINE PROVISION FOR CORRECTing what went wrong with humankind and what can move us forward toward the goal of fellowship with God. There is a clear dividing line between the Christian model and most other religious models because of our emphasis on God's provision of salvation, not on its achievement through human effort. As Paul says, we are saved by grace through faith, and as John says, we love God because of God's prior costly love for us (Eph 2:8-9; 1 Jn 4:19).

In part three we first consider what God provided by way of the sacrifice of Christ for our salvation. We explore why it was fitting that Christ should die for us (chapter nine). We wish to move our thinking about atonement from legalistic concepts to human and personal terms by seeing Christ's sufferings as God's sufferings for all those under the power of death. Thereupon we consider salvation as freedom and liberation (chapter ten) and baptism as a sacramental door of entry into a lifelong relationship with God (chapter eleven). Finally we take up the doctrine of the church as God's new community and redemptive bridge to the world (chapter twelve).

IX

SACRIFICE
Unconditional
Love

How is the relationship with god healed—how is fellowship with God restored? The Bible is a narrative of what God did to reconcile the world. The gods of other religions really do little to save in any deliberate way. The high god of the primitives, for example, lives far away and does little to help humans. The emptiness of Eastern thinking is not able to act, since the monistic absolute is not a person. Even in theistic religions, often God does not do more than make demands on people who need help. At most God may sympathize with our distress from a distance, but it is most rare to find God understood as One who is actually with us in our distress.

This emphasis makes Christianity special. According to the biblical witness, God saves humanity through the death and resurrection of Jesus Christ, God with us. Humanity has been raised from death to life in the person who acts as its representative. In Jesus, death is overcome and life is promised in the new creation. The representation of the one on behalf of the many is a key for understanding the cross and resurrection. Humanity endures death and judgment in the person of Christ, its representative. Through the cross comes a healing of the broken relationship between humans and God, and through the resurrection comes life and hope. As Paul says, having been reconciled by his death, we are saved by his life (Rom 5:10).

The God Who Initiates
The Bible presents a most surprising portrait of God. The gods of religion
tend to sit back and enjoy their status as gods. But God, according to the
gospel, is uncommon in that he does not remain distant, demanding better
performance. Rather, God takes the initiative to save sinners and, as the
prophet puts it, bares his holy arm:

> The LORD has bared his holy arm
> before the eyes of all the nations;
> and all the ends of the earth shall
> see the salvation of our God. (Is 52:10)

God loves us enough to get involved and do something about sin. He enters
into human suffering and redeems broken people. This was reflected in the
life of Jesus, who did not stay aloof but entered fully into life and all its pain.

"The Word became flesh and lived among us" (Jn 1:14). In a desire to save
humanity, God came among us to suffer and die for us. The heart of the
gospel can be put in four words: "God is for us" (Rom 8:31). God's will is that
sinners should live and not die. Therefore he invaded history, taking the
wrong of humanity on his shoulders, and put things right. God does not
stand on the sidelines but acts to heal the relationship we have broken.

God's Wisdom and the Cross
The cross is foolishness to Jews and Greeks, as Paul says, but to us it is the
wisdom and power of God (1 Cor 1:24). Where is the wisdom in it? Why did
God become human? Since God's wisdom is unsearchable, we do not expect
to find a completely satisfactory answer to that question. A rational explanation will fall short of being able to do justice to the wisdom of God. But since
faith seeks understanding, what light can be cast on the subject?[1]

A big problem in Western theology has been its preference for an abstract
legal theory of how the cross saves us. This has mightily influenced our
reading of the Scriptures and resulted in a strange view of God. It also pushed
aside the resurrection as a central event, since the theory had no real need
of it. The theory sees sin as a violation of justice and the cross as an infinite
propitiation and appeasement of God. On this view God easily becomes seen
not as the passionate lover of humankind but as an implacable judge and
avenger. This implication has burdened countless Christians and created

who knows how many atheists. Fresh thinking about the work of Christ is plainly needed.

When it comes to salvation, we must not see God as the problem. God is committed to saving us and does not need to be coaxed—even by Jesus—into loving sinners. The only problem is how to repair the broken relationship with humanity. Obviously, if God was in Christ reconciling the world to himself, God does not need to be reconciled to us—we need to be reconciled to him. The problem is how to get sinners to repent and turn from sin, to come back home and follow the new path of love.

According to the New Testament, God in wisdom chose the path of incarnation. God decided to become what he was not, to become human, the incarnate representative of all humanity. By doing so God would be in a position as man to surrender his will, resist temptation, suffer and die, rise and reign. As God and man, he could do that perfectly and vicariously for all of us. God could assume the brokenness in us that needs healing so badly. As man he could go through life, death and resurrection and then enable us to go through them. This is a major theme in early Greek theologians like Irenaeus: God took our humanity as its representative and obtained victory for us all.

The New Testament offers a number of images to explain what happened in Christ's death and resurrection, images that have been spun out into theories of atonement. One theory states that Christ was victorious over the powers of evil; another that Christ suffered vicariously as a sin offering for us; a third that the cross makes human transformation possible. The truth about Christ's work is many-faceted, and each of these interpretations has value, both as biblical interpretation and as possible explanation that we can use today. There is no reason to suppose one of them is true to the exclusion of the others and every reason to suspect each is true in some way together with the others. Each of the models says something important. God delivers us from powers of oppression, God frees us from the burden of our sins, and God strips us of our destructive illusions.

The Healing of Relationships

Creative love theism interprets the Christian message in the family room, not in a courtroom setting. We ask how the cross brings about the healing of relationships.[2] This approach avoids a mistake that has often occurred in the past, for it has been common to interpret the cross as needed to reconcile

God to humanity rather than humanity to God. St. Anselm (for example) saw humans as serfs of the Lord in a quasi-legal relationship and understood the problem of salvation in basically contractual terms. We have duties and obligations in relation to God, and having dishonored God through sin, we owe God a satisfaction. God cannot resume normal relations with us until this restitution is made. But since we cannot provide it, God sent Jesus to die and make the payment that would restore the Lord's honor. He makes it sound as if Jesus persuaded God to stop being angry and to start forgiving. What a strange idea of God compared with the biblical picture of him as a seeking Father! Besides, it creates new problems. What place is there for forgiveness if Christ paid the price? What an odd way to think of things.[3]

Calvin too thought in terms of payment and may have made the situation worse. For him God is not so much lord of the manor who has suffered dishonor as a stern judge who is angry with us and must be appeased. Calvin reasoned that Jesus sacrificed himself to appease this anger, make satisfaction and cause God to be favorable toward us. Calvin was a lawyer, and the thinking behind his model is legal through and through: In dying, Jesus addressed a tension in God's nature and resolved it. God was made favorable toward sinners by Christ's dying for them.[4]

The apostle Paul does not think in such terms. God himself gave Jesus up to death and provided a mercy seat that atoned for our sins (Rom 3:25). There is no thought of God's needing to be appeased before he could be gracious. The Servant of the Lord obediently pursued his mission to the bitter end out of his faithfulness to God. The Father was pleased, not angry, with him and through him was able to overcome the barriers to reconciliation.[5]

We have to overcome the rational theory of atonement, based on Latin judicial categories, that has dominated Western theology. It demotes the resurrection from its central place and changes the cross from scandal to abstract theory. It makes things sound as if God *wanted* Jesus to die and predestined Pilate and Caiaphas to make it happen. Surely not—Jesus is God's beloved Son. The Father and the Son are not divided or in opposition. In the giving of the Son, the Father is giving himself. As Jesus said, "Whoever has seen me has seen the Father" (Jn 14:9). In the suffering of Jesus we can feel the pain of the Father and the infinite grief of his love. The cross demonstrates the compassion of God. Through the surrender of Jesus, God seeks out lost sinners, enters into their forsakenness and brings them into an unbreakable fellowship.[6] Let us try to set our thinking about atonement in personal, not legalistic, terms.

The real issue is a broken relationship, not a breach of contract. Before the cross happened, God loved sinners and wanted to save them. The cross did not purchase love for sinners. It is we, not God, who need to be changed in attitude. The problem of salvation is our need to be delivered from the power of evil and become people who love God again.[7]

Let us strive for a relational understanding of the cross, in which we frame the problem as broken relationships, not divine anger and honor. God is healing relationships through this action. He is drawing wayward children home and re-creating right family relations. As in the parable, the father is already reconciled to the son and anxious only to welcome him home. The problem is that the prodigal is not yet reconciled to him.

Christ is not appeasing God's wrath. God is not sadistically crucifying his beloved Son. We are not talking retribution or criminal proceedings. The cross is a revelation of a compassionate God. Suffering love is the way of salvation for sinners. Jesus takes the pain of divine love on himself in solidarity with all of us. This tells us that God remains faithful to his creatures, even though they have abandoned him; he desires that they live and not die. This is how God justifies us and brings us back to life. The passion of the Father reaches out in the suffering of the Son, and the Spirit pours the love of God into our hearts.

We must realize that Jesus did not die in order to change God's attitude toward us but to change our attitude to God. God, who took the initiative of reconciling the world, does not need reconciling. It is in us that the decisive change is needed. The cross was not a sacrifice without which God could not love or forgive us; it was a sacrifice without which we would not have been able to accept forgiveness. The problem lies with us, not with God. He requires no sacrifice except a broken and contrite heart (Ps 51:16-17).

The real challenge is how to save us from ourselves, and the solution is incarnational. God elects to defeat his enemies by turning the other cheek, by accepting wounds inflicted upon him and making them the means of redemption. On the cross God absorbs all the hurt our sins have caused. Even as sinners drive nails into his hands, Jesus says, "Father, forgive them." Not lashing out, not retaliating, not holding out for satisfaction, God simply loves. The pain of the cross is the cost to God of restoring the broken relationship.[8]

The relationship is disrupted because we pursue our own interests. At its deepest level the problem is not corruption or guilt but alienation. We need to be penitent and turn from our wicked ways. God addresses this problem at the cross, absorbing the consequences of wrongs and suffering rejection himself. In the death of Christ, God commends his love toward us (Rom 5:8), and by means of it he breaks the power of evil over us (1 Pet 2:24). God wants the cross to have an impact on us. He wants us to change and live for righteousness.

Costly Forgiveness

The cross has an objective side too. When Christ died once and for all, he did something that made a difference independent of its impact on sinners. What objective status does the cross have in a family model? How does the cross change the situation for humankind?

It is possible to speak of propitiation in nonlegal terms. Forgiveness is costly to God. God also suffers to deal with the feelings that could have led to a rejection of humanity. Something happened in the life of God when he absorbed the pain and the judgment.

We must not forget the anguish and outrage God experiences in the wake of sin. The moral order is disrupted. But God's response to this is to let the consequences fall on him. He accepts them all—there is no need for any more suffering. This is the way God forgives those whose sins caused him to suffer. He forgives us as only an involved participant can forgive us, as One who was rejected on the cross.

God suffers in many ways. First, he experiences the consequences of sin as One who is totally good. Sin disgusts and affronts him. Second, as the lover of humanity God experiences the pathos of betrayal. Third, the Father suffers in the suffering of his Son, who was allowed to become the victim of sinners. The abused offered forgiveness to the abusers in an act of self-sacrifice. This goes far beyond sympathy. The wisdom of God takes the path that at one and the same time expresses disapproval of sin, demonstrates love, experiences the pain of betrayal and calls sinners to repentance.

It is love we confront at the cross, not wrath against us. When sinners put Jesus to death, it looked as though God disapproved of him. But God raised Jesus up and exalted him for the service rendered even unto death (Phil 2:9-11). This is not the picture of a God who is bound by justice, who demands a retributive penalty to satisfy him. The cross is the victory of love over that kind of retribution, not its vindication. Christ freely and willingly identified with us in our sinful condition, and his death was not an act of punishment but an act of solidarity that frees and transforms. Sin as betrayal is an offense against God's heart, not primarily against his justice or his honor. God is love, and wrath is the anguish of his love confronted by betrayal.

The cross is God at work in healing relationships. It is not a penal offering to reconcile conflicting dimensions of God but a loving sacrifice to bring the alienated home to love. The cross is God's way of overcoming love's anguish without indulging sin.

Jesus experienced abandonment by God on the cross. He glimpsed this coming abandonment in the Garden of Gethsemane when he asked that the cup might pass (Mk 14:36), and it came to expression on the cross in the mysterious cry of dereliction: "My God, my God, why have you forsaken me?" (Mk 15:34). The worst part of his torment was to experience alienation from God who loved him so. God did not even spare his own Son but freely gave him up for us all (Rom 8:32). Jesus experienced God-forsakenness and God-abandonment.

This is deepest mystery. It cannot mean that Jesus suffers while God sits back, indifferent and hostile. It can only be that the Father suffers with the Son, each in his own way. Christ is suffering the pain of dying, and the Father is suffering the death of his beloved. There are two experiences of divine passion, the passion of Christ dying and the passion of the Father letting it happen. In the pain of God the sin of the world is taken away. The Father and the Son together suffer the pain of God's love for the world.[9]

The Impact upon God

The cross has universal significance because it changed the human situation in a fundamental way. It has global meaning because it impacted God. In accepting the path of incarnation, God accepted human experiences that he had not undergone before. He experienced a genuinely human life, life in a body, and even death. At a certain point in human history, then, God suffered to forgive and to reconcile. The work of the cross was objective and has universal significance because it was objective in the very life of God. God immersed himself in the morass of human history to save us, apart from any response of ours. God had loved people, had forgiven sinners and had felt pathos before—but God had not suffered crucifixion until Calvary.[10]

By experiencing suffering as a human being by reason of incarnation,

God gained a moral authority and credibility in regard to overcoming evil in humans which he did not have before. In bearing our sorrows and becoming acquainted with our grief, God became a fellow sufferer and learned to understand us. A suffering God has moral credibility for dealing with our sin. The cross changed God, but not in the way we have thought. It did not change his attitude toward sinners from wrath to love. It did add to the divine experience, however, and qualified God to reconcile and transform sinners. God in Jesus died to sin and came to life to make salvation possible through union with him.

This is hinted at in the book of Hebrews. It confirms that through the incarnation God gained experiences that qualified him to save us (2:10, 17-18; 4:15-16; 5:7-8). By partaking in flesh and blood, he was made perfect through suffering and could overcome the power of death. Having suffered and been tempted, he is now able to help those who are tempted. He can now sympathize with our weaknesses because he was weak. Having become perfect, he became the source of eternal salvation and can lead us to glory. Hebrews confirms in these expressions that Christ was enabled to save us because of what he went through in life and death.

The point is, we think, that God entered history so profoundly that not only was the world touched and affected by it, but God was touched and affected by it also. God went beyond *showing* us that he loves us by actually *experiencing* evil and death in himself. Jesus took the place of the creature and became man in order (as man) to overturn our rebellion against God. He stood in our place, as our representative, and turned things around. He became one with us in his life, death and resurrection to bring about healing and salvation.

This is the heart of the Christian message. God took up the human cause because of his love for us, and he carried it through to the goal. God put us right and fulfilled our calling on our behalf. No other religion claims anything like this. No one else proclaims that God went through human experiences that qualify him alone to be the Redeemer of humanity.

It took a second Adam to make us what we were meant to be from the beginning: God's covenant partners. The Incarnate One embodied that goal for which we were made, and in union with the Son we can overcome alienation, submit ourselves to the Father and reenter communion with the triune God.

Jesus did not placate God or persuade God to be merciful. It was God's desire from the first to be gracious to sinners. The only question was how to implement mercy and bring about salvation. What would be the most fitting thing to do? Sin would have to be taken seriously; something would have to be done in place of a penalty; something would have to encourage us to stop sinning; something would have to impact God. God took care of all of this in the cross of Jesus Christ.

A Living Sacrifice

The biblical image of sacrifice addresses these issues. Sacrifice is basically an act of giving. Always thinking of sin offerings, we tend to forget that most of the sacrifices of the Bible are gifts of gratitude. By the mercies of God we offer ourselves in gratitude as living sacrifices (Rom 12:1). A sacrifice is an act of surrender and commitment to God. In the same way Jesus on the cross offered himself to God as our representative, to actualize in a vicarious way the full surrender that we had failed to offer. Therefore he calls us to die and rise with him to new life, and through him we offer sacrifices of praise to God (Heb 13:15).[11]

God's triune nature is relational and consists of giving and receiving. The world itself was made to reflect that reciprocal process, to provide an echo of the giving and receiving of the triune persons. Sin disabled the creature and spoiled our ability to present true sacrifices to God. It broke the reciprocity of giving and receiving that was intended. It was natural for God to heal the world by means of sacrifice, to manifest in Jesus' suffering a reciprocity in which the Father gives the Son and the Son renders a perfect offering of praise and obedience on our behalf through the Spirit (Heb 9:14). Now it is possible for the world, through the sacrifice of Christ, to offer creation back to God as a living sacrifice.

Christians believe God saves by means of sacrifice, but sacrifice is not a very meaningful category today. The idea of animals being killed and presented to God is a difficult, even repulsive, idea. Not that our own customs put us in a position to criticize the ancients. People in biblical times killed many fewer animals than we do and were more conscious of the sacrifice being made so that they might live. We hide all this from ourselves and think ourselves superior to them. Perhaps we should consider the possibility that ancient sacrifices were a symbol of humanness, not of barbarity. At least when the ancients ate meat, they were grateful to the animals from which it came, and to God as well.

At any rate, it helps to bring the category of sacrifice into the context of thankfulness. Sacrifice has much to do with giving gifts. True religion is bringing gifts to God, bringing the best that we have. Sin robs God of the gifts of thankful praise. Because the sacrifices we offer are so inadequate, Christ gave himself as a sacrifice to God. It helps us see that sacrifice in the context of giving and thankfulness, not only propitiation.

Because we neglect this motif, we also tend to miss the dimension of fellowship with the community. We forget that sacrifices were *eaten* after they were offered. The connection was obvious—the animal died that people might live. Even today Jews and Muslims pray when an animal's blood is shed. Sacrifice involved killing an animal for a family to eat. We have forgotten to think of meat-eating in this way. In our culture animals are just slaughtered out of sight and without prayer. Furthermore, we often just grab food and eat it alone. The sacrificial meaning is retrieved when we sit down and eat together, when we give thanks and remember God at the meal.

The meaning of sacrifice includes communion with God and fellowship with one another in eating. We are reminded of this in the Eucharist, when we participate in the sacrifice of Christ at his own table. The Lord's Supper is a fellowship meal where we eat together as God's family. It is a foretaste of the marriage supper of the Lamb and anticipates life with the triune God. Isaiah even describes salvation as a feast of "rich food" on the mountain of God (Is 25:6-8). Salvation can be depicted as table fellowship for all people, as a festive and joyful meal.

In most cultures people eat together in more than functional ways. In Western cultures, birthdays and anniversary celebrations, testimonial dinners, gatherings of leaders, wedding banquets, funeral wakes and the like retain social and ceremonial functions, and in them deeper meaning is attached to ordinary eating. In the Middle East the symbolic meaning of eating is still recognized as important. This recalls what meals were like in the first century, when Jesus was involved in meals and instituted the Lord's Supper. Recall the celebration when the prodigal came home, how the fatted calf was sacrificed and there was great thanksgiving and reconciliation in the family.

John's Gospel reflects on the theological importance of our eating together, giving what appears to be the longest account of the Last Supper but without actually describing the Eucharist itself (see Jn 6). We understand John to be wanting to place the event in the context of Jesus' ministry rather than seeing it as an isolated event at the end of Jesus' life on earth. No doubt he also wants to connect it to the breaking of bread and the feeding of the five thousand (6:1-14). His point is that from the miracle and in the Eucharist, Jesus feeds and nourishes us. The holy meal of the disciples is the food of everlasting life for us.

Sacrifice is not best understood in law-court terms. This distorts the biblical meaning. It is not basically a legal transaction intended to satisfy the justice of God. Sacrifice lies deep in the loving heart of God. In creative love theism we recognize that God is a triune unity of love. When God decided to include humans in the family, it involved accepting the pain of our betrayal and ingratitude. One who risks loving runs the danger of getting hurt. We hurt the ones we love: husbands hurt wives and wives hurt husbands, children hurt parents and parents hurt children, friends and lovers hurt each other. In deciding to create, God knew he could be hurt.

When we are hurt in loving, we often withdraw. But God's love is unconditional, and nothing diminishes his love for us. Grace is God's willingness to keep on loving in spite of everything. It is God's gift given at tremendous cost to his own heart. Each of the persons of the Trinity allows himself to be hurt by our sin and ungratefulness, but God's boundless grace assures us that we will be loved to the end without limit. Sacrifices were an attempt, then, to express commitment to God and symbolize God's acceptance.

Sacrifice is a universal category, but meanings vary. A sacrifice might be thought of as a way to force God to do what the worshiper expects. The prophets denounced those who assumed that sacrifices would be pleasing to God just because they were offered. In creative love theism, sacrifice points to the loving heart of God. It is not a means of earning God's favor or gaining access to God. Sacrifice is about the gifts of God and a reminder of God's willingness to be hurt and still keep on loving us. The Eucharist has nothing to do with forcing God to be gracious to us. The bread and the wine are not a repetition of Jesus' sacrifice. Sacrifice is from the heart of God, and as we accept and rely on God's sacrificial love we experience salvation. Communion takes up the essence of sacrifice in the giving and receiving of the bread and wine.

A Eucharistic Spirituality

The sacrifice of Christ has implications for spirituality. We encounter God in these physical signs. Ours is a material spirituality, rooted in the fact that the Word was made flesh. We rejoice in embodied existence and find our humanity not a barrier but a gateway to God. Taking the incarnation seriously also causes us to be gripped by love for the world, seeing in material things God's handiwork and in people the face of Jesus.

We practice a *eucharistic* spirituality, recognizing Jesus Christ in the bread and wine as well as in the lives of those who gather to partake. The meal signifies the sharing of God's life with the world and speaks of reconciliation as we break bread together, deferring to the neighbor and washing one another's feet. The sharing of bread is a sign of our humanity renewed in Christ. Sharing the food and fellowship, drinking the wine in the atmosphere of friendship, we engage in activities among the most meaningful in human life. We experience a foretaste and an anticipation of the new order symbolized as the banquet of God.

In the Eucharist, disciples share symbolically in the passion and death of Jesus. Holding to Christ crucified, we seek to follow him in the way of his cross. God entered the darkness of human suffering, redeemed it and has given it meaning. God gave up Jesus for us so that we might be free to give ourselves to others. His passionate involvement in the world promises to bring about transformation. We follow the Crucified One and are grafted onto his body. We worship a crucified God, put to death that we might live and share in his passion.

Paul writes: "Christ loved us and gave himself up for us, a fragrant offering and sacrifice to God" (Eph 5:2). He did on our behalf what we all should have done but could not do—present our bodies as a living sacrifice to God. Yet because of his death and resurrection in the power of the Spirit, because of our dying and rising with him, we may now humbly make our own sacrifice, holy and acceptable, which is our reasonable worship (Rom 12:1).

Jesus endured the worst that sinners could do to him, and God transmuted it into a mighty act of redemption. All the hostility and suffering of the world were upon him for the sake of our salvation.

X
LIBERATION
Freeing
Love

Life PROVES TO BE UNSATISFACTORY FOR MANY PEOPLE. THEY WISH IT HAD coherence and made sense but find it disordered and disrupted. They wonder whether there are any answers to the fundamental questions of existence, and they fail to realize their own potential. Secularism cannot help them, because it views life as a chance product of evolution having no destination.

The unsatisfactoriness of life gives religion a point of contact and an opportunity to speak of ways to restore meaning and hope. For Hindus, human misery is due to the conditions of a previous existence—one may hope for a better reincarnation next time. The Muslim, knowing that everything happens according to Allah's plan, must submit to God's will in every circumstance. Primitives know that misfortune is due to a neglected duty and resort to witch doctors to learn what action should be taken to remedy the situation. Each religion offers its adherents an explanation of the disorder and a prescription for a remedy.

Salvation is a broad concept in the Bible. A central theme, it covers everything from physical healing to the forgiveness of sins, from victory in battle to a new creation. The gospel is the power of God for salvation (Rom

1:16). God wants to deliver us from every evil that threatens our existence.

Being so broad a term, salvation can be approached from several angles. Evangelicals place the emphasis on the vertical relationship to God, justification by faith. Liberation theologians focus on salvation more in the sociopolitical sphere, viewing it as good news to the poor and deliverance from oppression. The category is comprehensive, so many applications are possible.[1]

Salvation has a broad meaning. Temporally it refers to something in the past (conversion), a process in the present (growth) and an event in the future (God's kingdom). Salvation encompasses concerns of both body and soul, individual and society, the material and the spiritual. It is inclusive of conversion, social concerns, healing, deliverance and even the regeneration of the universe. Salvation is about everything that is involved in the coming blessing of God's kingdom. Plainly, a holistic definition is required.

Salvation includes the healing of broken relationships—with God, with others, with nature. It includes the healing of persons, justice for the oppressed and stewardship of the natural world. It operates on many levels—spiritual, psychological, physical, economic, social and political. No aspect of the creation lies outside God's desire to bring restoration and wholeness. The church is called to participate in God's saving activity on behalf of this world through its actions and prayers, to strive for justice and liberation for the oppressed in every sense and to keep hope alive in people for the culmination of salvation at the end of time.

Salvation as Freedom
Paul likes to use the term *freedom* to explain what salvation means. "For freedom Christ has set us free. Stand firm, therefore, and do not submit again to a yoke of slavery" (Gal 5:1). Reconciled to God by faith, believers are free of bondage and free to be all they were meant to be. They are justified by faith, sanctified in love and called to a life of hope.[2]

Salvation as freedom begins with *justification,* God's acceptance of us despite our sins. The broken relationship is restored, and we are placed on the path to new life. We are freed from the necessity to justify ourselves, since we are accepted freely by grace. So however ordinary we think we are and whatever people say about us, we are all somebodies, not nobodies, because God accepts us. We have dignity and worth because we are loved by God. With this new beginning, the basis of our self-esteem, we can begin to live by grace through faith as we were created to do. Free from both presumption and sloth, we can learn to trust the benevolence of God again.

This freedom unfolds in the process of growth we call *sanctification*. This term refers to our being progressively transformed into Christ's image and likeness, which means living in the manner of self-giving, other-regarding love. As Paul says, "Those whom he foreknew he also predestined to be conformed to the image of his Son, in order that he might be the firstborn within a large family" (Rom 8:29). Believers are being conformed to the image of Christ through the power of the Spirit and God's sanctifying grace working in us.

Growth is needed in many areas. For example, we need to grow as hearers of God's Word and to mature in prayer. We need to be freed from the power of sin over us and to live in solidarity with our fellows. We need to abound in thankfulness to God and to live in mutually helpful relations with others. We are summoned to love and assist others, even our enemies, and to be among the first to promote justice, mutuality and friendship in society.

There is a third dimension besides justification and sanctification: *discipleship*. It is our vocation or calling to be God's witnesses to the coming kingdom and to be partners in the mending of creation. The Spirit is empowering us to engage in the struggle for renewal, to hope and to hunger for God's kingdom as we wait restlessly for it.

Paul says, "Where the Spirit of the Lord is, there is freedom" (2 Cor 3:17). The point is that salvation empowers our life and liberates us from all kinds of bondage. For example, it frees us from our anxiety, including the need to justify ourselves; it sets us free to struggle against evil both within and around us; it frees us of the ideologies that blind us to the evil that is working in our world. Because we are secure in God, we are set free to serve and free to risk.

Jesus preached good news to the poor and liberty to captives (Lk 4:18). Paul states, "The law of the Spirit of life in Christ Jesus has set you free from the law of sin and of death" (Rom 8:2). The Bible declares that God is liberating people who are in countless ways oppressed by sin and misery. We are filled with hope because we know that even the creation will be set free from its bondage to decay and obtain the glorious liberty of the children of God (Rom 8:21).

Liberation for the Oppressed

The category of *liberation* is biblical and has resonance within the modern consciousness. All over the world people are asking to be free of want, tyranny and oppression. The poor see that part of the world has risen out of poverty, and they want to participate in this process. In response, liberation theology has come into prominence. It calls on theology to be more than rational, more than mystical. Like James in the Bible, it calls on faith to do works. Theology ought to take a stand within historical struggles for justice. It ought to preach good news to the poor and not ignore their plight. It ought to speak about social justice and not justify the given order by its silence. We need a theology that arises from the experience of the oppressed as they read the Bible. This will add to our appreciation of Scripture's meaning and challenge us at many points.

Such theology may focus on racial, economic or gender issues. Black theology, for example, relates to the black experience—to issues of slavery, apartheid and racism. It calls black people to freedom, dignity and justice in the world. It hopes to impart hope and a sense of identity.

There are dangers in it. It is easy to fall into ethnocentrism and reverse racism. It is easy for opportunists to use it for their own selfish purposes. The gospel must never be used to bolster a worldly cause, however noble. It is wrong in the name of liberation to demand special advantages for black people, disadvantaging others. God transcends the political situation and judges all things.

Nevertheless, God cares about the suffering of black people, and theology is right to speak of human liberation.[3] Peace between tribes and races is an urgent problem facing the world today. Racism can be white, black, yellow or red—but no group is called to be permanent sufferers.

Latin American liberation theology focuses on the plight of poor people, not blacks or women. It pays less attention to issues of gender and race but interprets the gospel as good news to the poor addressing the situation of suffering. This theology is done in the context of poverty, using the language of revolution and radical social change. It speaks of God's preferential advocacy for the poor, claiming that God is on the side of the weak and powerless. Though it places its emphasis on salvation in this world, it does not necessarily deny other dimensions of salvation. It wants to say that salvation is both spiritual and material, for both body and soul. The mission of the church, therefore, is to contribute to the transformation of social conditions.[4]

Liberation theology has been successful in calling our attention to these issues, but less so in suggesting ways to actually improve the conditions of the poor. In calling consistently for socialist reforms over the years, liberation theologians have found themselves on the wrong side of analysis and reality. Practically everyone knows now that socialism does not work and why.

Nevertheless, liberation theology can make a contribution by calling attention to the plight of the poor and by aligning itself with a "neoliberal" strategy. That would be good for the poor and would ensure a future for liberation theology.[5]

The Old Testament prophets say that to know God requires one to seek justice and correct oppression. The Bible is greatly taken up with issues of justice in society. God desires justice to prevail in earthly societies, however imperfectly. Theology cannot be separated from this issue. Religion is not just a personal matter. Justice is central to the social teachings of the Bible, because we are called to reflect the fellowship of the Trinity, however dimly. We must be moved by the divine discontent about the condition of society as it is prior to the advent. To know and follow God requires us to pursue justice for all people, to struggle against racism, against every form of domination, in peacemaking (which may not mean pacifism) and in attempts to better the conditions of the poor.

God and Women

Feminist theology relates God and salvation to the experience of women. It is faith seeking understanding in relation to a history of women's being regarded as inferior because of their sex. It asks why power is always in the hands of men and why the feminine seems to be treated as only secondarily human. Feminist theology challenges the domination of men over women and promotes the full humanity of women. Whatever diminishes or denies this cannot be from God. We must regard women as fully human and not always subordinate. The aim of this theology is not to reduce men and have women dominate them or to deny important differences between men and women in their complementarity. Rather, the call is for a new partnership between men and women in which neither sex dominates the other or is the norm for the other. Feminist theology seeks a new relationship among human beings which incarnates mutuality. It would have men and women taking dominion over the earth together. It is as much about the liberation of men as of women—the one sex cannot be liberated without the other.

With the support of new exegesis, feminist theology presses for equal rights for women in church and society and opposes what it calls patriarchy. It fights for the dignity and worth of women and objects to men's treating women as if they were invisible. It wrestles with questions such as whether to regard men and women as very similar, opposing male privilege, or to stress how different men and women are, staking out special territory for women. The latter strategy risks justifying the status quo, since patriarchy can accommodate gender difference handily. But this strategy's realism makes it likely to win out against any unisex interpretation.

Feminist theology is also very concerned about the naming of God and seeks to recover feminine images of God in the Bible itself. The fact that the church tends not to make any use of the scriptural feminine images for God indicates that some change is called for.[6]

We must listen to the testimony of women who remind us of things forgotten and injustices long ignored. The Bible gives us the permission to name God in feminine ways. Feminine images may not be central, but they are surely present. God is One who gives us birth (Deut 32:18). God is like a female eagle bearing her young on her pinions (Deut 32:11). God is compared to a woman in labor (Is 42:14). God can no more forget us than a mother can forget her nursing child (Is 49:15). God comforts Israel as a mother carries her child on the hip (Is 66:12-13).

Greek Orthodox traditions have been more at home with female symbolism than have the Latin churches. Clement of Alexandria spoke of God as his father and his mother. He speaks of God giving us milk from breasts. Both Anselm and Julian of Norwich speak of the maternal aspects of God and Christ. Feminine symbolism is not foreign to Christianity, and the loss of the feminine has impoverished our understanding. We need the contribution of women's spirituality and women's experience in the understanding of God.

Thinking Liberally

Liberal theology is a theology of liberation too. As the name *liberal* implies, it is concerned about human freedom, specifically freedom from the bondage of tradition. Liberals want to be free to think for themselves and come up with new and better ideas. Why be in bondage to the past, if the ideas do not suit? Good tradition is one thing, ignorant prejudice another. We must be free to relearn and rethink. We must recognize our human limitations and not forget that ultimate meanings are mysterious, not easily grasped.

Theology ought to be creative, constructive and imaginative work.

This book is liberal in one sense—in critiquing traditions that do not do justice to what the Bible says and do not illuminate life today. But it is liberal in an evangelical way, in that its liberty is exercised in subjection to Holy Scripture.[7]

More Than Acquittal

Liberation is more than freedom from guilt, as in the forensic model, more than imputation, more than Christ's merit imputed to us in a legal transaction.[8] Justification itself is more than acquittal, having an eschatological, not merely forensic, meaning. It links us to God's putting things right in the future for us and for a wider humanity. The goal is victory over all hostile powers and the coming of the kingdom. When we believe in Jesus and are justified, we are incorporated into a new humanity that God has justified. Our justification is not a legal fiction that leaves us unchanged. It is also a matter of being caught in the flow of divine action that aims to bring righteousness to the world and transformation to us.[9]

"Christ" has become just a name for most people, the surname of Jesus of Nazareth, but it was originally a title with meaning. It identified Jesus as the anointed one, the Messiah who would come and change the world. The gospel of Christ is therefore a messianic proclamation that aims at both the reconciliation of sinners and the transformation of the world. Jesus is the Messiah who will redeem all aspects of the broken creation. This explains why he ministered to the oppressed, the sick and the poor. His goal is to heal all that is broken.

To follow Christ is to become a disciple and engage in work just like his. The goal of salvation is not just an otherworldly hope. It means to impact this world and introduces a process of healing in the whole universe.

The idea of liberation is found in other religions and ideologies. Personal liberation was always important in the East. In monistic philosophies, disciplines are prescribed for men and women to free them from the weary round of transmigration. Taoism offers freedom from rules and helps people flow with the natural order of things. In Buddhism freedom is defined as losing desire. In Zen *satori* is the result of a mental discipline that frees the mind from inherited ways of thinking.

There is both aptness and peril in using the term *liberation* for salvation. In recent years, many lost causes have been called and have called themselves liberation movements. Their proponents have sought to link their causes with Christian theology to make them respectable. Many have been deceived, and liberation has been given a bad name. Nevertheless, salvation is the liberating of people in history and in eternity and thus is consonant with political theologies that uphold democracy and freedom, gender theologies that celebrate male and female dignity and difference, theologies that speak to those who struggle with homosexulity.

The Jewish Passover pointed to liberation from slavery. Mary's Magnificat was a song about liberation. Jesus was not only speaking of spiritual blessings when he quoted Isaiah:

He has anointed me

to bring good news to the poor.

He has sent me to proclaim release to the captives

and recovery of sight to the blind,

to let the oppressed go free. (Lk 4:18)

We are beginning to grasp that freedom through Jesus is more than just the forgiveness of sin.

Christians need to think and speak of liberation. All too often God is thought of as suppressing rather than promoting freedom. He has been seen as a despot who models and sanctions oppressive regimes on earth, divine-right monarchies, clerical rule and patriarchal domination. Liberation theologies, despite their mistakes, have provided a healthy corrective to our too-limited focus on salvation as forgiveness and escape from hell. We need to bring personal piety, corporate worship and social action into a unified model of what God is doing in the world. The heart of creative love theism is that the triune God is love and has created us to share his love in freedom.

The Liberation of Love

Humans need to love and to be loved. We long for the intimacy of heart-to-heart conversation, but often find intimacy difficult to realize. We are fortunate if we have one or two friends with whom to share in depth. We are often not free to love as we would like. We are bound by childhood hurts, irrational fears, constraints of selfishness, legalism, pervasive social conditioning and structures of the world that inhibit our freedom to love and enjoy others.

At the heart of the need for liberation is a longing to be free—free to love, free to be with others, to listen to them and to cherish them. What we long for God also desires for us: to enjoy friendship, affection and community.[10]

The tragedy of slavery, oppression and prejudice is that people are not loving and conversing with one another. In Galatians 3:28 Paul mentions three issues of liberation in the early church involving ethnicity, social status and gender: "There is no longer Jew or Greek, there is no longer slave or free, there is no longer male or female, for all of you are one in Christ Jesus."[11] Liberation needed to take place; barriers had to be removed for love to flow between people of different races, social classes and genders. Paul is saying that we are free now to converse with people of other cultures, other social positions and the opposite sex.

Liberation means genuine communion. Ethnic, social, gender differences do not matter. We can engage in conversation with one another without letting the differences obstruct our relationship. When open communication happens between races, social classes and sexes, we experience a foretaste of heaven. Little children often seem free of the racial, class and gender barriers that imprison us, and we have longings for that kind of freedom ourselves, to become like little children.

Provisional and Permanent Liberation

Realistically, achieving liberation is impossible by our own efforts. There is a wide hiatus between the longing to be free and the achieving of freedom. We need God to be at work in us "both to will and to work for his good pleasure" (Phil 2:13).

Any merely human plan of liberation gets twisted by selfishness. History reminds us how revolutions that begin with a longing for freedom become sabotaged when the corruptions of power set in. We make a distinction between the healthy longing for freedom at the heart of a movement of liberation and its outworking in practice. God is on the side of freedom and is opposed to oppression, prejudice and patriarchy. Therefore we regard liberation movements initially in a favorable way. We try to include them in our understanding of what God is doing in the world. But at the same time, we insist that particular longings for freedom can only be satisfied in the bigger picture of God's liberation found in the gospel.

For Paul, freedom begins in the heart and is made possible by the Spirit. Liberation begins with the freedom to engage in conversation with the three persons of the Trinity and with the neighbor whom we encounter. Through the Spirit there is power to overcome a bondage of the will and to be free for intimate conversation, not only with God but also across barriers of class, race and gender. Spiritual reality is needed for all aspects of liberation, whether personal, social or political. Rather than the church opposing new movements of liberation, we believe that God is concerned about all the longings for liberation in our world.

A Patient Liberator
God is not only justifying us in a legal manner but is liberating us to become just and upright people. This justice includes the liberation of neighbors and strangers, foreigners and slaves, and all the oppressed of any race, class or gender.

We are all loved and forgiven because God's care for sinners is unconditional. The opportunity to be free among other free human beings, knowing that we are loved and forgiven before we even begin—this is good news indeed.

The beauty of it is that God is patient in his liberating of us. Paul expresses his gratitude to God in freeing him "even though I was formerly a blasphemer, a persecutor, and a man of violence" (1 Tim 1:13). He says that he received divine mercy because he had acted ignorantly in unbelief and that mercy overflowed into his life and changed him completely. God's search for us is most patient and merciful. One may say no to God a thousand times and still be forgiven and bathed in Easter life.

Liberation belongs not just to individuals but to the creation as well. We long for the time of peace and festivity that is prefigured in the sabbath rest that concludes God's creative activity. Just as the story in Genesis moves toward the goal of sabbath rest, so the whole world is now being moved toward the goal of a perfectly realized and fully enjoyed fellowship with God. Liberation is both exodus and sabbath: it is freedom from every bondage and freedom to live in peaceful community with God and every other creature. The sacrifice of Jesus Christ in which he gave himself up to God sets us free to love and praise God. It places us on a path of pilgrimage to the heavenly city and in a community that is being made new.

The psalmist says that God has set our feet in a broad place (Ps 31:8). God gives us living space far more generous than we could acquire on our own. Our sins crowd and compress us into narrow ruts and boring paths, but salvation places us in wide open fields. The Spirit leads us out of narrow places and opens our horizons, flooding us with life.

XI

BAPTISM
Invitation
Love

Having been set free, we acknowledge the rule of God in our lives through baptism. In this act we are received into the new community and the trinitarian fellowship of God. Baptism is the sign of our initiation and welcome into God's family. It publicly signifies that God accepts us, though we are sinners, and has incorporated us into the body of Christ. By baptism we enter a circle of communal life for nourishment and sustenance. We reenact the saving event of cross and resurrection, celebrating the love of God for all humanity. We also make common cause with all around the world who share the sacrament and become part of God's mission for discipling of the nations.

Baptism was authorized by the command of the Risen One and grounded in Jesus' own submission to baptism under John. By this act he entered into solidarity with lost humanity as its representative and began to live a life of costly service that would lead to his sacrificial death. In baptism we too begin a journey of faith with Christ in the direction of hope and the redemption of the world.

Sacrament of New Life

Baptism is the sign of reconciliation. Jesus died and rose to bring sinners to God, and in baptism he applies the fruit of his saving work to us. Those who were alienated from God are restored to communion. They are plunged into the loving grace of God, which pardons and cleanses. In baptism the old person dies and rises with Christ into new life. It is the first step toward sharing the life of the body of Christ, and is renewed daily as we take fresh plunges into the life, death and resurrection of Christ and are converted anew.

Baptism has many connotations and a rich set of meanings. No mere symbol, it is a sacrament of grace, and associated with it are many blessings. God wants to deal with us in baptism as we repent and put our trust in him. We enter into the new age of salvation and meet God as the Spirit descends on us (Acts 2:38). Baptism depicts sacramentally a dying and rising with Christ (Rom 6:3-4) as well as cleansing and the forgiveness of sins (Acts 22:16). Baptized into Christ, we put on Christ as a garment (Gal 3:27). By this circumcision made without hands, we put off the body of flesh (Col 2:11), are baptized into the body by the Spirit and drink of life-giving water (1 Cor 12:13). It is spoken of as the washing of regeneration and renewal of the Spirit (Tit 3:5). Peter says that we were saved through baptism—"not as a removal of dirt from the body, but as an appeal to God for a good conscience, through the resurrection of Jesus Christ" (1 Pet 3:21).

Baptism marks entry into the church. It is the decision to follow Jesus as disciple and the determination to walk in newness of life. The New Testament offers a variety of statements and images of baptism, and these have given rise to differing interpretations and emphases in the churches. Baptism is a purification, an incorporation, a new birth, an illumination, a consecration and a seal. Like Christ himself, the believer is anointed by the Spirit in baptism to share in the offices of prophet, priest and king. From baptism we go to proclaim the praises of God, offer up spiritual sacrifices and share in Christ's reign.[1]

Baptism and Discipleship

In Matthew's Gospel, Jesus says to his followers, "Go therefore and make disciples of all nations, baptizing them in the name of the Father and of the Son and of the Holy Spirit, and teaching them to obey everything that I have commanded you" (Mt 28:19-20). In this text, baptism (in addition to its other meanings) is seen as enrollment in the school of Christ. It makes people *disciples* of Christ and signals a commitment to live for him in the power of the Spirit.

This brings out the meaning of baptism as a moral act, as commitment to discipleship. (The Anabaptists have always seen baptism especially in these terms.) In baptism the decision is registered to submit to the way of Jesus Christ. After the first large group of believers were baptized, Scripture says, they "devoted themselves to the apostles' teaching and fellowship, to the breaking of bread and the prayers" (Acts 2:42). Paul picks the theme up in Romans, where after speaking about baptism he says, "Thanks be to God that you, having once been slaves of sin, have become obedient from the heart to the form of teaching to which you were entrusted" (6:17). There does not seem to have been a long period of instruction before baptism—rather, baptism came first and led to teaching and discipling. After being baptized, then, we are expected and enabled to walk in the new path.

Baptism marks the beginning of a new form of existence. Baptism not only declares that guilt has been removed but also speaks of our being released from the power of sin and death. To the question "Who will rescue me from this body of death?" Paul answers, "Thanks be to God! . . . The law of the Spirit of life in Christ Jesus has set you free from the law of sin and death" (Rom 7:24-25; 8:2).

The Christian life is a baptized life, the outworking of the redemption achieved in Christ. From that point we carry through the death and resurrection of Jesus in our lives. We have died, and our life is hid with Christ in God. Therefore we put to death what is earthly in us, put away foul practices and put on compassion and kindness. In baptism we appropriate new life and commit ourselves to actions that reflect newness (Col 3:1-11). Baptism and discipleship go together.

Baptism and the Gentiles

Jesus' promise to the nations is a theme in Matthew. While Jesus limited his ministry to Israel and forbade his disciples to preach to the Gentiles during his lifetime, he knew that Gentiles would share in the salvation of the last days. He and John the Baptist both warned fellow Jews that their own place in the kingdom might be taken by non-Jews.

> Do not presume to say to yourselves, "We have Abraham as our ancestor"; for I tell you, God is able from these stones to raise up children to Abraham. (Mt 3:9)

> I tell you, many will come from east and west and will eat with Abraham
> and Isaac and Jacob in the kingdom of heaven, while the heirs of the
> kingdom will be thrown into the outer darkness. (Mt 8:11-12)

Jesus knew the prophets' oracles that announced an eschatological pilgrimage of the nations to Jerusalem, and he spoke of this ingathering of Gentiles after the resurrection.

Jesus' refusal of a Gentile mission in his lifetime and his proclaiming of it after his resurrection are not contradictory. There is a proper order to these things, as Paul says: "to the Jew first and also to the Greek" (Rom 1:16). Jesus also went first to Israel, and after that an incorporation of the nations could ensue. After the blood of the new covenant was shed and a ransom was paid for the world, the kingdom of God in all its universality could come into play.

Once Jesus had preached to Israel and shed his blood, a new and inclusive people of God could be gathered, including men and women of every nation. Easter and Pentecost heralded the dawn of a new age in which the ingathering of the Gentiles is the central divine activity. The Gentile mission is part of the fulfillment of God's purposes, being the firstfruits of a new humanity. In mission we cooperate with God and anticipate a redemption in which all nations are welcomed at God's table, the veil is removed and death is abolished forever (Is 25:6-8).[2]

God said he would bless all the families of earth in Abraham (Gen 12:3). This blessing can now go forward to all nations because of Christ's ministry. The covenant with Abraham, given Israel's rejection of Jesus, will be fulfilled by the church as it goes into the world making disciples and baptizing. New converts can be incorporated into God's priestly people and, in turn, go forth to mediate the grace of God to the world (Ex 19:4-6; 1 Pet 2:9).

In Jesus' day teaching and discipleship were carried out by rabbis. Besides their public teaching, rabbis would gather a smaller number of disciples, and learning would occur within the relationship of teacher and follower. In ancient Greek cities one could study with a Stoic or Epicurean teacher; today in India gurus are surrounded by groups of devotees. Jesus called people to be his disciples too. The choice did not indicate an attainment on their part—they were simply enrolled and began a process of learning. The term *disciple* actually became a name for the early Christians: "it was in Antioch that the disciples were first called 'Christians' " (Acts 11:26). The church then consisted of ordinary people who had started to learn about the love of God revealed in Jesus.

This sheds light on the Great Commission to baptize and make disciples. The mention of the triune name in this commission is significant. New learners would be taught about the love of the Father, the grace of Christ and the fellowship of the Spirit. The trinitarian formula provided a kind of syllabus of the main areas of teaching that were needed. Since all baptisms recorded in the New Testament were immediate, without a delay for instruction, the baptized would not be expected to know a great deal before starting out. Having begun with faith, they could have their faith filled out and gain a fuller grasp of the truth afterward.

The Baptisms of John and Jesus

Baptism was the act by which John the Baptizer and Jesus enrolled their disciples. Water was an important symbol for them. There had been washings in the Old Testament which the prophets saw as symbolizing a clean heart. Jesus made the same point, that washing the outside of a cup is fine as long as the inside is washed too (Mt 23:25-26). Ezekiel hoped for the day when God would sprinkle people with clean water and put a new heart in them (Ezek 36:25), and Isaiah gave this oracle:

I will pour water on the thirsty land,

and streams on the dry ground;

I will pour my spirit upon your descendants,

and my blessing on your offspring. (Is 44:3)

It was expected that there would be a cleansing bath in the coming age of salvation. John the Baptizer picked up on this eschatological orientation when he called for repentance and baptism to prepare people for the coming of the Messiah. He thought baptism would prepare them for entrance into the messianic order when it dawned. Before Jesus came, John's disciples would have purified themselves by baptism to get ready for the Coming One. After baptism they would have been taught the lifestyle required by John.

People wonder why Jesus submitted to John's baptism of repentance. The answer must be that he came to his baptism, among those responding to John's message, to begin his messianic task as he understood it from the Scriptures. Jesus underwent his baptism not as a solitary individual but as one who was called to be Messiah and a representative for all humanity. So he undertook baptism on behalf of the world, just as later he would die and rise on its behalf. In baptism he took his place alongside sinners, as he would do later during his ministry. This act was the first step on the path of suffering destined for the Servant of the Lord. Through baptism he could declare solidarity with people in their need of deliverance and present himself to God for his task.

In his baptism Jesus received the Spirit and divine approval. As the bearer of the Spirit now, he was led forth to do battle with the powers of evil and to overcome them in the power of the Spirit. By the finger of God he would cast out demons and perform signs of the kingdom of God.

Like John, Jesus enrolled disciples during his ministry. Although in the Synoptic Gospels nothing is said of his baptizing them, it is clear in John's Gospel that he did so (Jn 3:22; 4:1-2). Jesus began his messianic work in baptism and had people baptized with a view to their entering the kingdom. This picture coheres with his call for baptism in the Great Commission. Had he not made use of baptism before, the Lord would have been calling for a new method of enrolling disciples, which seems unlikely. The book of Acts also shows Peter enrolling disciples by baptism without a hint that it was a new practice. So it is best to assume that Jesus enrolled disciples by baptism during his ministry and continued it after the Day of Pentecost.

Issues Surrounding Baptism in the New Testament
The parable of the sower explains why some of those baptized do not go on to become disciples, why though they have been baptized they do not continue in the teaching. Jesus describes some who begin with enthusiasm and quickly lose interest. There are others who are double-minded and have anxieties that choke the process of commitment. There are good and bad disciples, promising and unpromising ones.

Paul compares baptism to Israel's experience in the wilderness when they were "baptized into Moses" when they crossed the Red Sea. Though they ate the food and drink God gave them, many did not please God and were overthrown in the desert (1 Cor 10:5). Paul warns us not to be idolaters as some of them were. His point is that one may begin down the road of discipleship and not finish the course. John speaks of some attrition among the baptized, saying that many of them drew back and no longer walked with Jesus (Jn 6:66). Similarly, in his speech to the Ephesian elders Paul warns that some of the disciples will abandon their faith before long (Acts 20:28-31).[3]

As a leading rabbi, Nicodemus doubtless had disciples himself. When he sensed that Jesus was imparting something important, he was told that the way to learn would be to be baptized and then to learn more. A new birth would lead to a new process of learning. When Nicodemus objected that he was too old to start learning again like a young student in a school of discipleship, Jesus explained that he would need to be taught by the Spirit if he was to share in what God was doing (Jn 3:1-10).

We gain insight into how Jesus and his apostles may have viewed the effectiveness of the rite of baptism from a note in the Fourth Gospel. John tells us that after the first few disciples were enrolled, baptism was performed by the disciples, not by Jesus (Jn 4:2). Similarly, Paul says that he rarely baptized people himself but left it to others (1 Cor 1:14-17). This could have been owing to more pressing duties but may have been to avoid creating the impression that the baptizer or the baptism itself was the important thing, rather than the new life that was beginning and the new process of learning.

Baptism seems to have been performed rather quickly after conversion. There was not an extensive examination of candidates or a long probation. When the jailer repented in the middle of the night, Paul baptized him along with his family at once (Acts 16:33). The order was baptism, then instruction. This does not mean that baptisms were indiscriminate—repentance and faith were prerequisite. It simply underlines the point that those who were baptized were still only beginners.

Eligibility for Baptism

Jesus welcomed tax collectors and sinners into his circle. He was not picky about whom he accepted. The church too should be viewed more like an evening class for part-timers than a graduate school. In a night school one can easily enroll without any fuss, but there are numerous complicated preconditions if you seek to begin graduate school. The church is a school open to all and sundry. It offers instruction in what is involved in following Jesus.

The essential thing is not to check exhaustively the suitability and maturity of those who want baptism, but to make sure that they can be incorporated into the life and teaching of the congregation. Before we are taught, who among us is suitable? What is needed is faith in Jesus—the rest can come afterward.

This principle of baptizing converts immediately and leaving the Spirit to do the teaching after baptism is important. We should not require a high level of understanding and character before we enroll people by baptism.

Maturity comes later, after baptism into the community. The second-century practice of examining candidates thoroughly and requiring extensive probation before baptism is doubtful and something of a deviation. Surely the church is a school for disciples and baptism the way of enrolling the new learners.

What About Infant Baptism?
Brow, an Anglican, thinks children should be enrolled by baptism early in life so they can begin learning as soon as possible. Pinnock, a Baptist, believes in dedicating babies and letting them make their own mature commitment when they are older.

Supporters of infant baptism appeal to texts that speak of household baptisms, although they do not specifically mention babies. The decision may be a practical one, the question of how best to enroll learners. Why not baptize them and get them started right away? They can always decide later whether to continue. Alternatively, one could dedicate babies to this kind of life, bring them up in a Christian family and let them choose baptism when they are ready.

Baptists worry that baptizing infants is not really baptizing them. If baptism signifies dying and rising with Christ, washing away the stains of sin, being born again through the Spirit, incorporation into the body of Christ and the like, how can infant baptism be real baptism? If baptism means all this, what sense can it make to baptize infants?

We believe that the two forms of baptism together express a fuller meaning of baptism and that the best policy may be to practice them both. Like the Waldensians and certain Reformed churches, why not strike a compromise like the one in Acts 15? That story leaves no doubt that God is at work on both sides of the divide. On the one side, children are dedicated and brought up in the community; on the other side, children are pointed in baptism toward confirmation and a personal owning of faith at a suitable time. The goal of both practices is to enroll Christians as disciples, and this is what really counts. Why not respect one another's convictions and not require rebaptism of anyone?

The idea of baptism as enrollment is not meant to remove the mystery of the sacrament. It would do so if it were the only point of significance, but it is not. Commitment to being a disciple of Jesus is only one of the meanings of baptism.

Simple Yet Profound

Significant events can be very ordinary at first. Decisions to be married, to settle a large contract or to emigrate to another country—these are simple actions with enormous consequences. Such decisions reveal their significance over time. Baptism too is a simple act and may seem rather prosaic. We may hardly remember the circumstances of our baptism. But it has placed us in the church of Jesus Christ.

As we take our place there, we have the assurance that our sins are behind us and that failures will not exclude us in the future. The Spirit is eager to teach and help us to enter the mysteries of the kingdom. Wherever we go in the world, we have a ready place at the table of God's family as priests in the ministry of a local church community. Within the body we share experiences of joy, love, healing and worship as a foretaste of the glory already shared through the resurrection of our Lord Jesus Christ.

XII

CHURCH
Window
Love

BAPTISM ENROLLS US IN THE SCHOOL OF CHRIST AND INTRODUCES US TO THE fellowship of the church, the community that mediates his sacrifice to the world. We are called to this community not for special privileges but to be a priestly people that mediates between God and the nations. The church is a bridge over which the blessings of God flow to all the families of earth.[1]

Reconciled to God and restored to his family, we are part of a new fellowship. Not only do we enjoy a new status before God as individuals, but we are also incorporated into the body of Christ and made part of God's ongoing mission of reconciliation.

An Apostolic Church

Community is important to us, because we are social creatures made to reflect the relational being of the triune God. Ours is not a religion of the book so much as a life of faith and love lived in the community of the Lord whose Word is heard in the Scriptures and whose calling is to be an instrument of God's Word in the world. The church is an institution, a visible organization with activities that nourish the community and confront people with Christ. But at the same time it is a living *organism* filled with the Spirit.

This fellowship is an anticipation of the future, the firstfruits of a new humanity. As such the church does not exist for itself but for the world. Our task is to get the story right and to get it out. The church is not a fortress for keeping us safe but a consecrated people spread throughout the world to scatter the word of the gospel.

Beyond both institution and community, the church is a bridge to the world. It exists for nonmembers and, by reflecting God's love and participating in his mission, seeks to extend healing and hope to the world.[2]

The apostles were missionaries. When we say the church is *apostolic,* we mean both that it is founded upon the apostles' teachings and that it is commissioned to evangelize the world. The apostles had a unique witness. Theirs was the original testimony of Jesus, valid for all time and deposited in the New Testament. But the apostles were also sent forth into the world. To be apostolic also means having a commission to serve the kingdom of God among all nations. It means being sent forth as the apostles were, to be Christ's ambassadors with good news for all creatures.

Destined for communion in the fellowship of the triune God, we are also united on earth in a community designed to reflect God, whose triune nature underlines the centrality of church. In the church we begin to experience God's communal life with brothers and sisters. Called into Christ's body, we celebrate his love and share in his meal together.

God is calling a new community to be the foretaste of a new humanity. Transformed by the sacrifice of Christ, we too give our lives up for others. Called to reflect the Trinity, we live and minister in the mutuality of love that exists everlastingly in God. We image God himself as we place ourselves at the service of one another. A social God calls a community into being in order to embody the self-giving love that is at the heart of the trinitarian mystery itself (Phil 2:5-11).

Jesus and the Church

Jesus did not say much about the church in his lifetime, but he anticipated the church in his circle of disciples, a community in the service of the reign of God. Jesus spent his time proclaiming the kingdom, not thinking about the church. He began by preaching to Israel, hoping that the Jews might repent and return to their calling. Yet he did speak once about building a church in the future—see Matthew 16:18. It would be part of a long-term plan after his death and resurrection, when his followers would gather to remember him and preach the kingdom in his name. From his disciples a new community was born at Pentecost and began to live in anticipation of the kingdom.[3]

Jesus would not have wanted his church to point to itself, because in itself the church is weak and fallible. Rather, he would want us to look to God's kingdom, which stands forever. The church's task would not be to control history but to serve the needy in his name. His followers would be serving God whenever they served men and women freely, as Christ had served them. This church would be called to selfless service, without protection of dignity and rank, and would embody the salvation of sinners just as he did.

Not a staid organization, the church is to be a dynamic organism embodying God's love and hastening toward the kingdom. The church is a pilgrim people being led by God's Spirit into the future. Although operating under certain forms of social existence, it must remain flexible in the freedom of the Spirit to be able to adapt to changing circumstances. Its mission and effectiveness are not due to its human resources, which are not special. Paul says that not many wise and rich have been called (1 Cor 1:26). Success will be a matter of God's strength being made perfect in weakness. As the prophet said, it is not by might nor by power but by God's Spirit (Zech 4:6). The church participates in a movement of peoplehood that began with the call of Israel, had its breakthrough with Jesus Christ and now is to bring God's touch to the whole world. Church life and mission are meant to be "a demonstration of the Spirit and of power" (1 Cor 2:4).[4]

Israel and the Church

After the golden calf incident in the wilderness, God questioned whether he would be able to accompany the Hebrew people any longer. He suggested that it might be better if an angel went with them and if he stayed at a distance, for fear that if he got too close his anger might be kindled against them. Moses protested this idea on the grounds that the original vision had been for Israel to be a priestly people whose distinctiveness would be God's presence with them (Ex 33:16). So Moses would settle for nothing less, and he prevailed with God. Only a church with the presence and power of God can fulfill the mission God has given.

Basic to Israel's identity was its call to be the people of God. God pledges over and over: "I will be your God and you will be my people" (as in Lev 26:12). Christians do not carry Israel's name. Israel is and will remain his people, even after the resurrection, even in unbelief, because the gifts and calling of God are not canceled (Rom 11:29). Even when Israel is unfaithful, God remains faithful (Rom 3:4).

The church, however, is an extension of the principle of peoplehood embodied in Israel. We have been grafted to the vine and become a new expression of it (Rom 11:17). Hebrews 11 traces our history back to the beginning of time. The church was made necessary by the sin and backsliding of Israel. As those who put faith in him, we have inherited God's promise of a new covenant. As Gentiles, we are free of Jewish legislation and anticipate the ingathering of the world's peoples.

In relation to Jews today, we share Paul's sorrow about them (Rom 9:1-5; 10:1). We know that God wants them to receive Jesus as their Messiah so that he can have mercy on all (Rom 11:32). Our relationship with the Jews of today is one of friendly competition. The Jews ask for evidence that the Messiah has come into the world, which appears to them unchanged. We must try to give such evidence to them. Paul speaks of making Israel jealous of what we have received from God in the wake of their rejection of Jesus (Rom 11:11, 14). We do this when we bear convincing witness to the fulfillment of prophecy in Jesus and when it becomes evident when we are truly converted and are serving the kingdom of God.

The Concept of Church

Like many other biblical teachings, *church* is a rich concept. Scripture uses dozens of images to describe it: temple, people, fellowship, priesthood, flock, army, school, hospital and more.[5] The word is a translation of the Greek term *ekklēsia* and has an originally secular meaning. It could refer to an assembly of citizens, such as the group that came together in Ephesus in Acts 19:32. It could refer to a town meeting where citizens gathered to carry out community business. A feature of Hellenistic civilization was cities' government by such public assemblies of citizens. Our term *church* retains something of this idea of a gathering to conduct God's business. More important is the fact that the word was used in the Greek translation of the Old Testament for the Hebrew word *congregation,* referring to Israel.

One metaphor for church is God's temple. The Spirit of the last days was poured out on the community, forming it into a shrine or earthly residence of the risen Lord. As we are filled and gifted by the Spirit, Peter encourages us:

Like living stones, let yourselves be built into a spiritual house, to be a holy priesthood, to offer spiritual sacrifices acceptable to God through Jesus Christ. . . . You are a chosen race, a royal priesthood, a holy nation, God's own people, in order that you may proclaim the mighty acts of him who called you out of darkness into his marvelous light. (1 Pet 2:5, 9)

The apostle is thinking of the congregation of Israel that came out of Egypt at the exodus and were told that they were "a priestly kingdom and a holy nation" (Ex 19:6). The whole people were to be priests, with the Levites serving as their representatives and others appointed to serve the tabernacle and temple (Num 3:7).

The epistle to the Hebrews explains that Jesus Christ has become the high priest of the new covenant, and all his people share the priestly office with him. There is not be a distinct priestly class in the church, since all God's people are priests. For this reason the term was not used for any church office in New Testament times. Jesus performed the priestly function and calls us all to share in his priesthood. Priesthood includes having access to God in prayer and offering up sacrifices of praise. As priests we preach the Word and point one another to the One who has indeed called us out of darkness into light. Clergy are not the only priests in church—the ministry of the whole people of God is priestly.

It is the same with the *people of God* category. All the faithful belong to God's people, and we should not drive wedges between them. There is a basic equality among believers, so that no special class of clergy ought to be exalted over ordinary members of the church. That does not mean there can be no differentiations whatsoever of role or function. That would be too radical an inference. All Christians should testify, for example, but not all of them minister the Word. All sing hymns, but not all are trained to sing solo parts. In any congregation some are able to do more than others in certain areas and may be set aside to perform these functions. This contributes to good order.

Should churches wish to ordain priests, however, it should be understood that all share in priestly functions with them. We are all to carry out the tasks of priests on behalf of the world.

As priests, we should be human and accessible rather than remote. It should be easy for ordinary people to talk to us and to confess their sins, failures and frustrations. Priests should not be easily shocked, and they should be able to give absolution. What is told in confidence must be kept secret. Having heard the person's story, the priest should express the need in prayer to God. Teaching of the Word is also required, and a priest should be able to do that. There are also ceremonial functions, and on some such occasions the priest's most important role may be simply to be present. God's priests should be present like salt and leaven at every occasion and in every place to celebrate or mourn, to comfort or rebuke. Priestly functions can be performed by ordinary Christians, and they should be encouraged to do so.

The Work of Ministry

Paul says that all the saints should be involved in the work of ministry. Gifts of leadership are given to equip them for ministry (Eph 4:11-12). The church is strengthened as God's agent of mission when we have this reformation of church life.

The ministry of all believers, male and female, is an urgent piece of unfinished business. All Christians need to see themselves as a channel through whom God would work and mediate his life to others. The church should not be pastor-focused but people-focused. Everyone in the church organism is called to be a player in God's mission. Christianity is a lay movement, and its ministry is the expression of the giftedness of the body. It is imperative that we all see ourselves as gifted people, called to mission and ministry.[6]

The church has a gift structure by which it lives and works. Gifts are for everyone, not a select few. Not all gifts are unusual or extraordinary, though some are. Alongside prophecy and miracles are gifts of service and mercy. We should be open to all of the diverse gifts, while remembering that the element of service is basic to them all. Gifts are intended to channel love to people who need it. They exist for the good of the community and, beyond that, for the good of the world. If the gifts of the whole community could be fully actualized, dynamic power, life and movement would be released.

Women as well as men are called to assume leadership. Women belong to the royal priesthood and share in the gifts of the Spirit. From the beginning women were ministers in the church and coworkers with the apostles (Rom 16:1-16; Phil 4:2-3). The reason for this is simple: by baptism both men and women are joined to the body and are called to minister in his name. Women are to be included in every form of ministry and not arbitrarily excluded. Ministers represent the congregation before God and ought to represent the wholeness of the family, made up of male and female.

We are not just responding to modern pressure—there are good reasons for ordaining women. Let us not confuse social customs that can be changed from time to time with issues of the faith itself. Women are equipped naturally and supernaturally to preach the Word, to administer the sacraments and to care for souls. It is an offense and a waste of talent to deny them these opportunities.[7]

United as Friends of God

Christians should be caring, loving people who are willing to serve every community. Rather than being separated from others, singled out as "the saved," they should be seen as friends of God and humankind. Instead of viewing the church as the lifeboat of the redeemed, we ought to view it as a royal priesthood existing for the world. "Outside the church there is no salvation" is a negative axiom. We would do well to substitute a positive statement: "Inside the church there is good news for everyone." Through Jesus Christ the whole world is graced. We must not exclude sinners but offer selfless and unpretentious service to the world. The church is a window into God's love, an open community of people dedicated to work for the salvation of all.

Paul gave his life to opening windows to God's love. After fifteen years of church planting, he said, "From Jerusalem and as far around as Illyricum I have fully proclaimed the good news of Christ" (Rom 15:19). He spread the good news over a territory stretching fifteen hundred miles and including great cities. He could not convert everyone in all these areas but did plant priestly communities, churches to serve as windows into the love of God. In the power of the Spirit he established holy priesthoods in every center. He engaged in strategic church planting with the salvation of the whole world as his goal.

Church division is a serious problem today. With so many denominations, people understandably wonder which one is the true church. Diversity is not in itself a bad thing and does not change the fact that we all confess one Lord Jesus Christ and are one at a deep level. There were different kinds of churches even in the New Testament. The mere existence of different types of churches does not contradict the unity of the church in and of itself.

What does contradict unity is coexistence without love or cooperation, where we confront one another in hostile ways. Differences between churches become harmful when they exclude. There needs to be a growing together in love toward one another if we hope to impress others about the truth of the gospel of Jesus. Jesus prayed, "I ask not only on behalf of these, but also on behalf of those who will believe in me through their word, that they may all be one. As you, Father, are in me and I am in you, may they also be in us, so that the world may believe that you have sent me" (Jn 17:20-21).

Beyond coming closer in spirit, we have somehow to get back behind the ancient schisms and heal wounds. We must become more visibly one and work at finding common ground. Let us see ourselves as community with other communities, confessing one Lord Jesus Christ and partaking of one sacred meal. Like the early churches that sent gifts of love to poorer churches, let us give concrete expression to our unity. We must cultivate unity in our diversity.[8]

The Reformation addressed real abuses in the church and made needed corrections. But the idea behind it was reform, not fragmentation. The intent was not to split the church forever. If the schism was needed then, it ought to be transcended now. Reform is not meant to divide permanently. For all the gains of the Reformation, there were also terrible losses. The trend has been to more and more fragmentation and to the loss of more and more of the ancient jewels of church tradition. Nowadays people do not even recognize the treasures of their own tradition. If a Christian practices meditation, for example, others suspect a New Age influence, forgetting the Orthodox and Catholic traditions of contemplation.

A divided church means divided truth. It means that a denomination will be strong in one area and weak in others. It means not being able to find the fullness of church in any one stream. It has also fractured the authority of the church to speak out on issues of faith and morals. Our divisions have led to subjectivist theologies.

The day has come for us to be evangelical-catholics. Let us go back before the schisms and recover what was common to us all. Let us recover the treasures we have lost. Those of us in the free churches need to reclaim some of the things we foolishly discarded: the ancient practices, the fathers and the mothers of church tradition, the Christian year and the lectionary, the spiritual disciplines and church order, sacramental life and liturgical worship. Why impoverish ourselves any further? Others will need to work for renewal in mainline churches. Those in the free churches can more readily rediscover the treasures of the historic churches when they sense that the catholic side is attentive to the Word of God and respectful of the gifts and ministries of the Spirit.[9]

PART FOUR
Doctrine
of
Faith

GOD CALLS US INTO FELLOWSHIP IN HIS NEW RECONCILED FAMILY. HE SUM-
mons us to a transforming friendship and grants us the privilege of
participation in the mutuality of the triune society. In part four we
turn to the spirituality of creative love theism, to the kind of life that
moves us toward the goal of loving fellowship. God who first loved us
calls us to love him in return. He calls us to be his friends in a
relationship that grows and deepens. Love cannot be coerced; it must
be invited. God invites us to a free, interactive, loving relationship with
him.

Once saved by grace, we are called to live by faith, a life of simple
trust in the goodness of God extended to us. From there we are called
to live in love, in the spirit of mutual caring that reflects the purpose
of our existence: to mirror the social Trinity. We also live in hope,
longing for the coming of the kingdom and restless for the comple-
tion of the work of redemption. Faith, love and hope are the chief
expressions of the new humanity, because they indicate the way to be
newly human by the grace of God in Jesus through the Spirit.

Faith expresses the thankfulness we feel for what has been given
and gives opportunity for petition in the activity of prayer (chapter
thirteen). Our friendship with God leads us into a lifelong process of
healing and into holiness (chapter fourteen). We are nourished by
feeding on God's Word (chapter fifteen) and refreshed by the fellowship of other believers (chapter sixteen).

XIII

PRAYER
Conversational
Love

Faith is more than a once-and-for-all decision. It has a beginning—some can remember the very moment when they turned to God—but, more important, it is a path and a direction. Once a baby is born, it wants to grow. In the same way, having begun in faith, we get moving in the direction of God's light and presence. Job was a pagan when he began his faith journey, but where he began was less important than the direction he was going. The goal of faith is a transforming fellowship with God, a life process in which Christ is being formed in us (Gal 4:19), a process in which faith expresses itself in love (Gal 5:6).

The Faith Journey

A person can be quite religious and yet be traveling away from God. In commending sinners who believed, Jesus was really saying that however far away from the kingdom they might appear to be at the moment of faith, they were moving in the right direction, which is the important thing. He castigated Pharisees because though as pious Jews they were near God's kingdom in one sense, they were actually quite estranged in their hearts and were moving further away from God. A person who has never read the Bible or been inside a church may have a heart that is open to God and that pleases him. God looks for faith in us more than for theological knowledge. We are saved by faith, not by what we know (Heb 11:6).

In terms of experience, faith is an awakening to God, when we recognize our Savior, feel sorry for what we have done and experience thankfulness for the new relationship offered us. It makes us free to be human, to give ourselves to God and live a life of love that corresponds to the love of the Trinity. The path of faith is a twofold movement of love toward God and love toward our neighbor. It requires us to put God and God's cause first—that is, the cause of reconciling and restoring human beings.[1]

Because creative love theism focuses on reconciled and restored relationships, it implies a certain kind of spirituality, one of growing in friendship with God. Remember that Jesus calls us friends: "I do not call you servants any longer, because the servant does not know what the master is doing; but I have called you friends, because I have made known to you everything that I have heard from my Father" (Jn 15:15). God does not subordinate us or leave us in the dark about his plans. He has always wanted us to be his covenant partners. Thus there are no "little people" in God's sight; we are all precious and important to him.

Called to fellowship with the triune God and reconciled to the family of God, we have a Father in heaven who loves and cares for us. Jesus himself knew he needed to deepen his relationship with God, when he went away to a quiet place to commune with God. He gave time to this relationship and waited on God.[2]

Our relationship with God is not primarily a legal one. An acquitted man would feel grateful to the judge who pronounced him not guilty, but would not necessarily love the judge or want to be his friend. Interpreting religion in a calculating way, in terms of imputation and legal fiction, does not leave enough room for loving devotion. When we emphasize the legal, prayer becomes more a duty for pleasing God than a delight at the heart of the relationship. In rationalistic religion the brain may find satisfaction, but the heart is left cold.

Prayer is central to creative love theism because God made us conversation partners. We are God's friends and need to have a heart-to-heart relationship with him. Prayer is a basic expression of our faith. Close friends talk often and spend time with one another; conversing is central to friendship. So our relationship with God cannot be healthy if prayer is incidental to it. Prayer mediates our growing in a love relationship. Those who love well pray well; those who love little pray little.

Our culture is seeking an intimate relationship with God. People crave warm, mystical faith, not cold rationality and formal liturgy.[3]

The Life of Prayer

Prayer is our answer to the gifts God freely bestows on us. The Spirit within us stimulates joy and gratitude and unites us to Christ in our prayers. It is God's way of bringing us into greater intimacy with himself. Through prayer we enter into God's plans and cooperate with him in his work. Our prayers are always answered, though not necessarily in the exact ways we envisaged. God takes them seriously and weaves them into his plan for the salvation of humanity.

Effectiveness in prayer is not automatic. It is an exercise to pursue and an area for Christian growth. Maturity in prayer is important because it is an expression of our intimate relation to God. Christians must talk and pray *to* God, not only *about* God: We need to increase in love and zero in on the work he is doing in our lives and in society. We need to become better attuned to his voice as he summons us to acts of love and obedience. We need to learn to be honest in our praising and in our crying out to him. We need to distinguish between what we may want and what we really need.

Prayer is a basic exercise of our faith and the key to a transforming friendship. It is a primary expression of our faith because it is our communication as sons and daughters with our God. We are persons, not objects, to God. He has freed us from sin to be his covenant partners. He desires our conversation, our spontaneous gratitude, even our questioning and protesting. In prayer we place our entire existence in God's hands.[4]

The Christian life is union with Christ. Much more than judicial acquittal, it is deeply mystical. Paul even identifies the riches of the gospel as "Christ in you, the hope of glory" (Col 1:27). Elsewhere he testifies: "I have been crucified with Christ; and it is no longer I who live, but it is Christ who lives in me. And the life I now live in the flesh I live by faith in the Son of God, who loved me and gave himself for me" (Gal 2:19-20).

We Christians are much too rushed and busy. We do not give enough time to meditation and contemplation in our union with Christ. Andrew Murray, in unanimity with all mystics, urges us to learn the secret of waiting on God, because friendships take time. We have to slow down and focus on God's presence and on his working in our lives.[5] We need to wait on God in silence and cultivate a deeper relationship with him.

Because God is present with us, we need always to be drawing on his presence. The psalmist says, "For God alone my soul waits in silence, for my hope is from him" (Ps 62:5). We engage God with the heart, not only with the mind. As we remember that God is continually with us, at the center of our being, we let ourselves be drawn into his presence to experience his love.[6]

Prayer is also a necessity because of all the foes, dangers and temptations that we face. The Christian life is a conflict and involves spiritual warfare. Therefore we ask God to help us remain faithful to him. We pray, "Lead us not into temptation." Besides a way to cultivate friendship, prayer is a weapon in our warfare (Eph 6:18).

Charismatic and Contemplative

Recent years have witnessed a surge of charismatic spirituality that tends to be outspoken, demonstrative and affective, with singing, dancing, tongues and prophecy. It would be a cold heart indeed that does not detect in this movement a release of the Holy Spirit into human experience. The fruit is fairly abundant—praise and adoration, spontaneous testimony and expressive bodily action, an outpouring of love and spiritual ecstasy. Many people are being set spiritually free and overcoming their fear of Easter life. They are realizing that more things are possible with God than they had thought. This glorious awakening of charismatic experience is reminiscent of the book of Acts.[7]

Why do some have difficulty receiving this fullness? Jürgen Moltmann comments:

> The essential impediment to the charismatic experience of our potentialities for living is to be found in our passive sins, not our active ones; for the hindrance is not our despairing attempt to be ourselves, but our despairing attempt not to be ourselves, so that out of fear of life and fear of death we fall short of what our own lives could be. The charismata of the Spirit are present wherever faith in God drives out these fears of life, and whenever the hope of resurrection overcomes the fear of death. According to the testimonies of the first Christians, it was the Easter jubilation over Christ's resurrection that released the stream of charismata in the congregations. The pentecostal movement begins at Easter.[8]

Charismatic expression *and* contemplative prayer should be integrated in our practice. As in the whole of life, so in our spirituality: there is a time to speak and a time to keep silent. It is common after the experience of strongly affective prayer to feel a hunger for quietness and solitude. As the renewal matures many are being drawn into contemplative prayer, for the two are complementary. The outpoured Spirit opens us up to deep union with the Risen Lord as well as to exuberant praise.[9]

The prophet tells us, "The LORD is in his holy temple; let all the earth keep silence before him!" (Hab 2:20). The psalmist writes, "Be still, and know that I am God" (Ps 46:10). A too-active people, we need to center in and listen to God. The contribution of charismatic renewal has been to awaken Christians to the dynamic activities of the Spirit. But sooner or later it is necessary to introduce periods of silence and move into contemplative expressions of prayer also. The renewal will realize its potential as it opens itself also to the traditions of meditation.[10]

God is longing for us to come "higher up and deeper in" to his heart. He would sing his love song over us if we would but open the door of our heart to him. God aches over our absence and our distance from him. He mourns when we do not move toward him. God's heart is open and wants to deepen our friendship. Knowing God is not merely a matter of having a new status—it is coming home to the Father.

Reading Scripture as Prayer

One way to enter into God's presence deeply is through what has been called divine reading, or lectio divina. This is a devotional kind of reading that employs Scripture as a means of grace. The issue is not *how much* but *how* we read the Bible. The idea is to read only a brief passage, slowly and meditatively. This way we do not merely skim the surface of the text; we begin to go deep into its content.

So often we read the Bible for information rather than for transformation. We may be seeking data for a systematic theology or a prophecy puzzle rather than seeking the person of God. We forget that Scripture is God's love letter to his people more than a legal brief or encyclopedia.

The secret is to go off alone by yourself, get still and listen to God. Read a brief passage of the Bible slowly, and let it soak in. Enter into the mystery of the gospel, go to the heart of the subject, allow God to touch your life. Turn mere reading into conversation as you pass some time with God.

Prayer is an intelligible activity because ours is an open universe, not ruled by fate. As coworkers and partners with God, we are actually given a role in shaping the future. Prayers are actions that God weaves into the course of events; he takes seriously what we pray for and cares about what we are concerned with. He answers our petitions on his own timetable in his own way, if they are in the direction of his kingdom. He even modifies his own actions to take us into account and prefers to do nothing himself that he can delegate to us or to others.

Thanksgiving Prayer

Christians need to mature in joyful thanksgiving prayers because we serve the Lord not with superficial cheeriness but in deep gratitude for our friendship with God. There is much to be sober about in this world, of course, but we are thankful because we believe that divine grace will ultimately triumph over evil and death.

Thanksgiving is basic to prayer. Even those who express doubts about God and the possibility of relationship with him still know how to say thank you. They may not admit that it is God they are thanking, but it is hard to be thankful to chance or matter or even a creative force. It is not easy to be an atheist when you feel thankfulness coming on!

Thanksgiving is a response to grace. There is no room for it in the type of religion in which one earns salvation. It arises when we sense that we are experiencing something good and undeserved: when we respond to the beauty of creation, the delight of family and friends or any of the tender mercies of God. The term *eucharist* derives from the Greek word for grace, and we call Communion "the Eucharist" because it is an expression of thanksgiving for God's love and grace. The Eucharist unites the individual thanksgivings of the community and, by focusing them in the sacrament, strengthens worshipers to be even more thankful.

Thankful people are a joy—they have an inner sweetness that invigorates others in the home, the workplace and social gatherings. People without thanksgiving can be crabby and unpleasant, but thankful people sweeten the social space.

Prayer and Sacrifice

Sacrifices to God, though often thought of as ways to placate the deity to obtain favors, are actually acts of thanksgiving in response to God's acceptance of us. For Christians, sacrifice focuses on reconciliation. Since the death and resurrection of Jesus, animal sacrifices have been replaced by Communion, where people fellowship around a table and remember God's self-giving love.

For an ordinary meal to be possible, normally the life of an animal is sacrificed. Love between persons is also sustained by sacrifice, by a willingness to be hurt. Children only realize later in life how much it cost their parents to love and care for them. The triune God too is hurt in the course of loving us—each person of the Trinity feels the hurt and the pain.

When we get hurt in relationships, we often introduce conditions to avoid such pain in the future: We say, "I will love you again if you are sorry and promise to act differently." God's sacrificial love involves him in a continual willingness to absorb, forgive and forget the hurt of loving.

Our experience of prayer relates to the sacrifice of God. At first we have little conception of the sacrifice that welcomes us into trinitarian conversation, but every now and then we have an experience that enables us to understand it better and sparks a gratitude that enriches our prayer life. Prayer is based on sacrifice and enriched by further conversation that brings us into the heart of God.

In prayer God invites us to share the sacrificial love that he has for us. While we, like other animals, are willing to sacrifice for our children, we do not find it easy to extend unconditional love to others. Paul puts it realistically: "Indeed, rarely will anyone die for a righteous person—though perhaps for a good person someone might actually dare to die" (Rom 5:7-8). God is seeking to draw us into ever more costly love. When we engage in acts of kindness, when we find ourselves helping a needy person at some cost and even danger to ourselves, a window opens for us into God's love. Once the first step is taken, we do not know how far it will take us, but it moves us down the path of Calvary.

Prayer and God's Plan

Some are concerned about prayer's relationship to the decisions we make. They may assume that God has a detailed plan fixed and laid out and that they have to find out what it is and carry it out point by point. But trying to find out in detail what God has ordained, even regarding major decisions, is difficult and can become an obsession that paralyzes us.[11]

It is wiser to think of God as having a perfect plan, but not in the sense of a detailed blueprint. God's plan is a general one: for us to be set free to love.

God is not the sort of monarch who has to run our lives for us. He is a fatherlike king who includes us in his business, gives us areas of responsibility and risks our making mistakes.

In the parable of the talents, servants are given money to invest according to their ability. They are not told how to invest it, whether in a train of camels or in the grain trade. They are free to invest it however they choose. The one thing required is that they not be afraid to take chances and that they not be afraid of their master. Had the third servant invested the money and failed, the master would have commended him for trying and would have given him more to invest (Mt 25:14-23).

Faith involves risk. It is faith in the Father's love that frees us to take the risks of loving, and prayer is the way we share these plans with God. Sometimes God gives us clear direction, but often he wants us to take our own initiative.

In the same way, Scripture offers no normative pattern, no blueprint, for governing the church and carrying out God's mission. We are expected to find creative ways to love God and humanity and to operate with the prayerful confidence that God will lead us into the future. Many social services in the modern world began because Christians took the risk of opening hospitals, orphanages, leprosy colonies, institutions of education, shelters for the abused, churches among remote tribes, aid projects and the like. Faith in a loving God has produced and still produces a variety of risk-taking actions in the service of others.

Intercession

Genuine love for others leads to prayer on their behalf. Almost anyone whose child is in danger will express concern by sighs from the heart, even though such prayer may lack focus. Because we participate in a loving conversation with God, when we really care for another person it is natural to express our concern in prayer to our Father. We say, "Father, this is one of our family. You care about her even more than we do, and we pray for your hand of blessing upon her."

We also talk to Jesus about people in need: "This person needs your friendship and support. He is gripped by guilt and needs your forgiveness. Help him to enter into your sacrifice and find the peace of being willing to be hurt in forgiving his parents."

Conversation with the Spirit in prayer may focus on the deep sources of the person's feelings: "She needs your inspiration to see more clearly what is upsetting her. Please comfort and console her." We speak to the Spirit about issues of character—love, joy, peace, patience, kindness, goodness, faithfulness, gentleness and self-control. We speak about spiritual gifts needed for a particular kind of service.

The whole Trinity is involved in our prayer conversation. God is not impassive but is affected by our concerns. When a real prayer conversation goes on, the divine power of love is released.

Meeting in people's houses was a practice of the early Christians. Much pastoral care and loving service can emerge from such group meetings. In this context Christians can readily learn the simplicity and effectiveness of simple conversational prayer. As we pray together, we learn to look beyond a perceived need and discern the need for God's work in the person's social setting. Many people need liberation from feelings, situations, family relationships or systems that hold them captive. As several believers bring together their concerns and insights, they learn to leave matters in God's hands.

A Family Conversation

There are no unheard prayers. All prayers are heard, even if all are not granted. It would not be good for God to grant all petitions. Often what we think people need is not actually best for them. The timing or the approach may be wrong. There may be a need for delay or for the concern to be met in a different way. Since God is loving and wise, we assume by faith that when the story is finished, we will have received more and far better than what we had asked.

It is hard to imagine how God can hear the prayers of every person. But if humans can design a computer for a banking system that can process thousands of transactions per second, the Creator of the universe can surely relate to each person.

In conversational prayer we are not trying to force God's hand. We keep bringing loved ones to God until we see how the need should be fulfilled. We may find that since we talked to God yesterday, the situation is clearer and the need is cast in a different light. In prayer we listen to what God is saying to us. We have the assurance not only that God is hearing and responding to what we say but that he is addressing us as well.

Parents talk to a newborn baby even though it probably understands little of what they say. They say how beautiful it is, how bright, though the child hears only sounds. Eventually distinctions are made and phrases begin to make sense. In a few years the child can engage in fairly complex conversation. Learning to converse is a skill that has to be learned. In a similar way it takes time for us to hear what God is saying.

A mother conveys her love to a child by various avenues. She can speak, sing, hold, hug, feed, massage and kiss the baby. The child learns to interpret her facial and body language. Understanding the mother's verbal communication takes longer.

According to creative love theism, God loves us and is concerned to foster love in everything we experience. He seeks to speak to us nonverbally through sunsets, trees, daffodils, a singing bird, flying gulls, a baby at her mother's breast, children playing, lovers hand in hand, a smile, a greeting, a hug. God communicates verbally with us through Scripture, conversation, books, films, newspapers. We hear God speak through the experience of opposites: joy and pain, kindnesses and insults, justice and oppression, good sex and bad sex, sickness and healing, the good and bad consequences of behavior, the fear of death and the readiness to die. As we have these experiences and find ourselves talking to God about them, we slowly learn how to interpret God's language.

The Bible helps us learn the language of God. For those unable to read, God's words are heard in public worship, in the oral reading and exposition of Scripture, in the washing of baptism and sharing in the family meal, in marriage and burial services, in fellowship, prayers and singing.

Prayer is our conversation with God, our Parent and Friend. In prayer the Spirit communicates with our spirit. The experience can be powerful and astonishing.

Because God is our Father, prayer is never a work to earn his love. Though an autistic child may never be able to respond to conversation, the parents love and accept him or her. Nevertheless, all parents long for the conversation of their children. And even more than earthly mothers and fathers, our heavenly Parent waits and listens for the voices of the children he loves.

XIV

HEALING
Transforming
Love

SALVATION IS THE HEALING OF PERSONS. ITS GOAL IS RESTORATION OF THE image of God in us by the power of the Spirit. God's eternal purpose is that we be conformed to the image of Jesus, who is the true likeness, that he might be the firstborn among many brothers and sisters (Rom 8:29). As Paul says, God "chose us in Christ before the foundation of the world to be holy and blameless before him in love" (Eph 1:4). Salvation is a lifetime process that issues in resurrection, the day when we will be like him and see him as he is (1 Jn 3:2) and be changed into his likeness from one degree of glory to another (2 Cor 3:18).[1]

Salvation is a large category. The psalmist indicates this when he writes, "Bless the LORD, O my soul, and do not forget all his benefits," and then goes on to make a long list of them: forgiveness, healing, deliverance from death, renewal of strength, liberation, pity and so on (Ps 103). Salvation addresses nothing less than the whole person, which is many-sided. Humans have many dimensions—body, mind, emotions, spirit—and experience brokenness in every one of these areas. Salvation must address every facet of our need; it cannot have a narrow meaning, because God is intent on saving the whole person. Salvation covers the field from holiness to resurrection—if it did not, it would not address the full extent of the problem. It is a process of restoring wholeness to persons in body, mind and spirit. True spirituality is life-affirming and life-saving, not negative or cramping.[2]

The Cure of Souls

One basic goal of salvation is restored relationships, with God vertically and with one another horizontally. God wants us to be Christlike in every situation. It takes a moment to be born again but a lifetime to grow up into maturity in Christ. The Book of Common Prayer expresses our longing: "Almighty God, unto whom all hearts are open, all desires known, and from whom no secrets are hid: cleanse the thoughts of our hearts by the inspiration of thy Holy Spirit, that we may perfectly love thee and worthily magnify thy holy name; through Christ, our Lord. Amen."

Basic to healing salvation is the transformation of character. God is ever with us, and we need his power to help us rise above lust and pride. We need God to teach, empower and love us through the whole process. We are comforted to know what John writes: "The one who is in you is greater than the one who is in the world" (1 Jn 4:4). But growth in holiness also takes effort on our part. Baptism enrolls us in a school for discipleship and holiness. We have to learn obedience as Christ did from what he suffered (Heb 5:8). Battling with the enemy of our souls, we form good habits of the heart by practicing the classic spiritual disciplines.

We are enrolled in an educational process designed to refine and purge, toughen and mature us. We have to be brought gradually into moral and spiritual shape. Growth occurs as we develop holy habits and make use of the disciplines. There are ways to strike blows against pride and increase the enjoyment of a meek and humble life. We are pilgrims on a journey of becoming more loving and godly persons; we are spiritual athletes entering training to develop our abilities.[3]

Psychology is a modern form of the ancient art of caring for souls. There is always a need for mending the inner life and nurturing the center of affections. We respond to God's concern for persons when we help people deal with pain and grow in responsiveness to God. Jesus saw each person as precious in God's sight. He gave them time and listened to the needs of each. He responded to each person according to his or her need, whether it was physical, moral or spiritual.

Caregivers today can look to Jesus as a model, considering his self-assurance, his love and empathy, his wisdom and tact, his fidelity and integrity, his candor and realism. Pastors are gifted to attend to the care of souls in a special way, but we are all called to care for one another.

Salvation of the Corporate

Holiness is not only individual and private; it spills over into social concerns. Our concern for transformation overflows into concern about the world around us. This is unavoidable. Since all persons participate in the structures of a larger world, persons and structures are inseparable. There cannot be real transformation unless the world is transformed as well as individuals in it. Just as there cannot be complete salvation without resurrection, there cannot be full salvation without the liberation of creation. The renewal of persons is part of the renewal of all things (Rev 21:5). The whole creation must be set free (Rom 8:23).[4]

For this reason, personal holiness naturally issues in social holiness. Indeed, there is a social justice tradition of Christian spirituality. Beyond exercises for the devout, the way of holiness takes us into passion for the transformation not only of persons but of institutions as well. With Jesus we must stand against oppression in the power of the Spirit and speak out for liberation, giving voice to the voiceless. The yoke of bondage must be broken and idols spoken against.

The church influences the social order by fostering the values of the kingdom of God and by creating a moral environment. We do this not out of civic duty but out of our love for Jesus. We identify with his concern for the needy not because we have to but because we want to.

We see some of this in our society. Sin reveals itself in destructive patterns, but sometimes another pattern breaks through. A kingdom pattern is evident where there is concern for the sick and the poor, where the divine pretensions of the state are rejected, where service and humility are valued, where people call for the honoring of human rights and where democratic freedoms are granted. Wherever the way of Jesus has had influence among many people in a society, real progress has been made and we can see a degree of social sanctification.[5]

Healing for the Sick

The Lambeth Conference (1978) stated, "The healing of the sick in [Jesus'] name is as much a part of the proclamation of the kingdom as the preaching of the good news of Jesus Christ." Indeed, healing needs to be restored to its place as a normal part of the church's ministry. God gives life to our mortal bodies in advance of resurrection (Rom 8:11). The Spirit of life is present in the church, gifting people in diverse ways. In each one the Spirit comes into visibility in both everyday and special ways (1 Cor 12:7). God is a vitalizing energy—in him we live and have our being. The Spirit creates a climate of Easter life.

Along with his proclamation of the gospel, Jesus healed the sick as testimony to the presence of the kingdom of God. Healings of mental and physical illnesses were signs of the new creation. The sick came to him in their weakness; Jesus confronted the powers of death in them and released the energies of the Spirit in healing and deliverance.[6]

The notion of God as a healer was already familiar from the Old Testament. God said to Israel, "I will not bring upon you any of the diseases that I brought upon the Egyptians, for I am the LORD who heals you" (Ex 15:26). The psalms include a variety of prayers for healing (such as Ps 38:3-7; 103:1-5).

Through Agnes Sanford, Francis MacNutt, the Order of St. Luke and many others, healing is being restored to the ministry of the churches.[7] Healing is becoming a regular part of congregational life. In the Vineyard movement, healing has become central once again.[8] Ordinary Christians are being encouraged to develop gifts in this area.

Doctors do not really heal—they remove obstacles to nature's own healing energies when they correct a chemical imbalance or remove diseased tissues. Similarly, when faith touches the human spirit, it releases God-given forces within the body.

Varieties of Healing
There are many kinds of healing ministry. There is the healing of memories, for example. Just as there are blocks to health in the physical realm, there are blocks in the realm of the personality, creating a need for inner healing. Such obstacles may be moral, in the form of sin unrepented of. Or there may an emotional disturbance due to past hurts. Inner healing exposes the causes of such pain and releases the sufferer from the weight of the past. Prayer can free people from this captivity. It can probe the soul and help open a place for God's healing to enter. A closer union with God in the depth of the spirit can bring about an integration of the individual around a new center.

Many forms of disease in people are due to a sick society. The social environment may help or hurt us. People get caught up in destructive situations and stand in need of new community. The church embodies a witness to social brokenness, being itself a center of support and healing where true community can be experienced.

There are many ways to reaching out to the sick and troubled in the name of Christ: the Eucharist, anointing with oil, laying on of hands, reconciliation of enemies, casting out of demons, and more. Practically everyone can be part of an active healing community. The power to heal is not limited to a special class of Christians. Love is a healing agent, and anyone who loves contributes toward healing of others. On the other hand, just as some are more gifted as preachers than others, God uses certain individuals in the ministry of healing in special ways. There is certainly no basis for supposing that gifts of healing ceased when the New Testament canon was closed.[9]

Christians do well to form the habit of blessing people in the name of the Lord. In this way we ask God to help them in every aspect of their lives. We should always be expressing concern for the health (in the broad sense) of others. God heals all sorts of people in all sorts of areas by all sorts of means. It can even happen to our enemies. Jesus said: "Pray for those who persecute you, so that you may be children of your Father in heaven; for he makes his sun rise on the evil and on the good, and sends rain on the righteous and on the unrighteous" (Mt 5:44-45).[10]

Every disease should be brought to God with a view to wholeness. The ministry of healing makes use not only of normal medical means but also of every spiritual, psychological and social means that is consonant with biblical teaching. Faith is important in the healing of relationships, memories of childhood traumas, alcohol and drug abuse, and discouragement because of failure, unemployment and dependency. Faith can introduce wholeness into every situation.

We recognize secular agencies as allies in the various ways in which God liberates and heals us. But Christians add to their efforts the dimension of faith in a loving God. Beyond the normally recognized means of helping people find healing, we believe in the Spirit's everyday healing influences and in his special actions to heal the body or mind.

Though God heals in special ways, the sick should be encouraged to use all normal medical means of treatment. Christians involved in ministries of healing should never disparage the work of physicians, discourage the use of prescribed drugs or suggest a contradiction between faith in God and faith in a doctor. The various avenues of healing are all complementary.

The Healing of Guilt and Addiction

Faith is important in accepting forgiveness, but it is also needed in the reconciled community. Medical reports show that unresolved guilt can cause all sorts of abnormalities of body and mind and that we need healing communities to enable people to accept forgiveness and live without crippling guilt. We need churches that do not moralize and load people with guilt that makes them sick. Because we celebrate Jesus' forgiveness, we can offer liberating words to those who have been wracked by obsessive guilt feelings.

People also fall into destructive addictions. An addiction is a compulsive behavior that traps a person. But grace can heal when persons are assured that God understands and forgives them and will help them find a way to escape. The key is to look to God rather than focusing on one's own inability to perform. Alcoholics Anonymous has had success in helping people to look to God for this kind of healing. It shows the healing power of words of encouragement, backed up by the concern of a group that accepts the person as one of them. Healing is found in an accepting God and a loving community.

The Healing of Emotions

In our day, increasing numbers of people identify themselves as victims of childhood sexual or other abuses. Here too, a welcoming community of friends who listen is an important ingredient in healing. Persons burdened by shame need the resources of faith to accept forgiveness for their imagined or real complicity. For complete healing, the abused will need to become able to forgive the parent, relative or stranger who abused them. They may need the help of a counselor to help them face and deal with the trauma. In a community of mutual forgiveness they may see that the sin that hurt them can be forgiven and healed. They learn to trust in the power of God to overcome their inability to forgive.

Understanding that God himself accepts being hurt by our sin gives us a reason to travel the same path. When we are willing to absorb and let go of the sin that hurt us, rather than trying to make the other person pay, there is power to forgive. We might even be able, like God, to remember the sin no more. Such a willingness to let go of sin is the best cure for the hatred, anger, jealousy and resentment that cause many physical and spiritual ailments.

Research shows that some (by no means all) cancer patients are people who have long felt hopeless and despairing. The onset of the disease can be associated with a series of losses. Cancer has physical causes, but it may be abetted by discouragement and the breakdown of relationships. In such cases inner healing has a role to play. Faith in a loving God who has a creative purpose for every person is an ingredient for healing. The healing process is enhanced when the sick person is a member of a faith community in which the contribution of each individual is highly valued.

Healing can be sought through simple prayer or along sacramental lines. Many in ministries of healing find that Communion can powerfully focus faith in the healing power of Christ. The laying on of hands for healing in the context of sharing in the bread and wine can be very powerful.

Faith for Others

In certain Gospel accounts a person's healing depends on the faith of others. One such case is the healing of a paralyzed man. In Mark's account of it, four men removed roof tiles and lowered the paralytic man on a pallet so that he could be in the presence of Jesus. All three Synoptic Gospels say that it was the faith of these four friends, not the man's own faith, that saved and brought him forgiveness.

Had guilt for something he had done in the past caused his paralysis? Since Jesus offered him forgiveness before physical healing, it seems as if the guilt had to be dealt with before the healing could occur. The man was healed when he had faith to respond to Jesus' command to take his bed and go home.

Why was the faith of those who brought him for healing so important? Think of the faith of parents as they take a sick child to the doctor. The story of the paralytic and other accounts of healing strengthen our faith and help us to visualize ourselves bringing someone to Jesus to be healed.

People should be encouraged to bring their friends, whether they have faith or not, to services of prayer for the sick. Those who want prayer for any kind of sickness in body, mind or emotions, whether for themselves or for others, are invited to come to Jesus to be touched by him.

Listening and Laying On Hands

The Gospels tell how Jesus *touched* lepers and *touched* the eyes of the blind. In the ministry of healing, the laying on of hands in Jesus' name is often an aid to faith and a means of healing. Sometimes the transference of healing power can be sensed. Even without any unusual manifestations, however, touch has a way of communicating God's love beyond words.

Anointing with oil has been prescribed as a means to use in healing ministry (Jas 5:14-16). As laying on hands symbolizes Jesus' healing touch, anointing with oil symbolizes the healing work of the Holy Spirit.

Just listening can be a healing action. A person with no psychological training can help heal many kinds of emotional disturbance by listening. In one sense this is easy, but it can also be hard. The difficulty is that we get impatient and want to give advice out of our own agenda. We need to believe that people can be healed by God as we stay with them and give them our close attention. As soon as possible, though, the person should be encouraged to express his or her feelings and concerns in conversational prayer with God.

Beyond prayer, the healing of a troubled person is enhanced by engaging in human conversation, as a one-sided listening opens out into mutual interaction. The object of effective listening is to free the troubled person from dependence on the listener. Those who struggle need to depend on God and be sustained by the community. What difficulty counselors have who leave God and the church out of their therapy.

Some Are Not Healed

God can heal everyone, but all are not healed in this life. Stephen and James were martyred; all the apostles died with their generation. In each case, no doubt people prayed for healing or deliverance from death. Perhaps some of these leaders were anointed with oil and had elders come and lay hands on them. It is not true that if there is enough faith, physical healing will always occur. Paul himself was not healed from his thorn in the flesh (2 Cor 12:7-9).

Here is a motto for the disabled: "For we are weak in him, but . . . we will live with him by the power of God" (2 Cor 13:4). There is a gift of handicapped life. The power of God does not despise but makes use of weaknesses. In any church there are whole and infirm, wise and foolish, strong and weak. All are valuable to the community, and none can be dispensed with. Each has his or her charism in the body of Christ. The strength of God works in every disablement; any life shines when the love of God falls upon it. We need both weak and strong members in the body of our crucified and risen Lord.

For each person this is true:

Those who wait for the LORD shall renew their strength,

they shall mount up with wings like eagles,

they shall run and not be weary,

they shall walk and not faint. (Is 40:31)

God loves us all and has made us for resurrection. Everyone will be perfectly whole and healed in the end. But the sequence and timing must be left to God. God's timetable may seem slow by our reckoning. But we *will* receive the healing we need for our work on earth, and we will receive the remainder through death.

Doctors are trained to think that the object of their practice is to prevent death at any price, but that is not so. Partly through the work of the hospice movement, the importance of dying with dignity is now being recognized. Heroic methods of keeping the body alive at any price can no longer be accepted. There is a time to live and a time to die. But whether we live or whether we die, we are the Lord's and destined for new creation.

XV

BIBLE
Feeding
Love

NEARLY EVERY RELIGION HAS A CANON OF WRITINGS THAT ARTICULATE THE revelation of a community and instruct believers. Gathering inspired texts together and honoring them as scripture is a universal phenomenon. Such documents enjoy a special status and are regarded as deriving from a divine breathing.[1] Religions that worship a personal God have a special regard for revelation deposited in scripture because of the interpersonal conversation at the heart of their model. Creating a scriptural canon is the best way to conserve the treasure of revelation in history and transmit its insights to succeeding generations. To have these insights objectified in holy writings prevents them from fading in memory and being misrepresented.[2]

The Christian Revelation
Faith recognizes that scripture gives access to revelation and to the community whose scripture it is. The sacred books convey the theological model of faith and shape believers in it. Christians will not feel as nourished by the Gita or Buddhists by the Qur'an as they would by their own scriptures, because the other scriptures are alien to them and do not convey their own

model of faith. Believers more naturally turn to the scriptures that convey and nourish them in their own model. Not that there is nothing to be gained from reading the scriptures of other communities. There is enough common ground to make the exercise edifying, and it is also useful for interreligious dialogue.

The Bible is the foundational document of the church, and its revelation is transmitted through this witness. The category "Word of God" is larger than the Bible, referring as it does to Jesus himself and to the word proclaimed, but God's Word is uniquely mediated through the writings that function to mediate a saving encounter with God.

Claims for the inspiration of Scripture in the Bible are practical and functional more than theoretical. Paul speaks very practically when he says that the Scriptures were given by the Holy Spirit to instruct us for salvation and to equip us for good works (2 Tim 3:15-17). His emphasis is on the profitability, not the inerrancy, of the text, for he sees Scripture more as a means of grace than as an encyclopedia of information. Despite the humanity of the witnesses, the Bible is supremely profitable and shapes our lives. The apostle does not encourage us to speculate about inspiration but to profit from Scripture.[3]

The Bible does not occupy the central place in Christianity that the Qur'an occupies in Islam. For Christians the Bible is subordinated to Jesus Christ, who alone has center stage. The Bible is not like the Qur'an, alleged to be a perfect book dictated by God, untouched by any human or historical factor.[4] The Bible is a more ordinary book and plays a more ordinary role. We preach Christ from the Bible, not the Bible as such. While inspired by the Spirit, the Bible is an anointed human testimony to Jesus Christ, a treasure in earthen vessels (2 Cor 4:7). The humility that placed the Son of God on a peasant woman's breast, allowed him to be arrested as a common criminal and had the gospel proclaimed in a vulgar tongue—this divine humility chose to give God's Word in ordinary human forms.[5]

Protestant confessions declare the Bible *infallible* for faith and life. This is a book that does not fail us. An ordinary ruler is good enough for the work that children do but not infallible enough for making engineering drawings. The best ruler is crooked when compared with a laser beam. The issue is not whether the Scriptures are inspired and infallible. The question is what sort of authority they have and what sort of truth they convey. Knowing this helps us make the best use of these resources.

What Is the Bible For?

Evangelicals have spent a good deal of time and energy defending the inspiration of the Bible. It is time to give more thought to the Bible's function. In defending the Bible we may have left the impression that it is a book only for skilled apologists and expert interpreters. What is the function of the Bible?

The Bible is a book that feeds and equips the believing community.[6] It is a source of sustenance as well as a deposit of truth. The Spirit inspired Scripture in the past to be God's instrument in the present, an ever-fresh revealing of God for those on the pilgrimage of faith. It is so much like a sacrament that we wonder why, as the theology of sacraments developed, Scripture was not set among them. Certainly the Bible has been a primary vehicle of grace and blessing to the saints. From it we have derived the content of faith, receive instruction and are nourished. Along with the incarnation and the church itself, we might consider the Bible a fundamental sacrament underlying the others.

Religious ideas are easily twisted, and ideas about the purpose of Scripture certainly fall into this category. People have the strangest ideas about what the Scriptures are and how they function. Some think the King James Version is the original Bible. Others use the Bible as a storehouse of proof texts for constructing doctrine or projections of future events. Moralists use it to create systems of law, and the hardhearted employ it as a weapon against their enemies.[7]

We need to remember that the purpose of the Bible is practical. It was not given to be a source of systematic theology. The Bible was given to the community as a source of authority and as nourishment for its life with God. It nurtures a liberating relationship with God in a variety of ways, thanks to its rich diversity—through narratives, prophecies, wisdom and teachings. We believe not in the Bible but in the living God attested by the Bible. We celebrate the power of this book to nourish life in relation to God and others. The Bible is a rich and diverse witness that draws us into the story of redemption and into living out that story ourselves.

Interpreting the Bible

How do we interpret the Scriptures? First, making use of the tools available to us, we try to discover what the original authors were intending. We uphold the primacy of their intended meaning because we respect these writers as inspired by God and want to know what they had to say. We want to discover how God's truth was actualized in their hearing.[8]

Second, we read Scripture as witness to the saving activity of God. It tells us how God's purposes are being worked out in history and puts us in touch with the Christian story. God who created heaven and earth has done mighty things for humanity, and the biblical narrative tells us who we are and gives us an identity in the new community. We can never exhaust Scripture, but we can continue to penetrate it.

Third, we read the ancient text in our modern context, straining to hear what the Spirit is saying now and open to what God is doing in our day as he makes all things new. The Spirit uses the Bible to move us forward toward the heavenly city. We have to be careful not to allow our prejudices to get in the way of hearing the Word. It is easy to notice only what we want to hear. To counter this (at least in part), we should listen to others in the community when they tell us what they are finding in the Bible. We may receive from them interpretations that have thus far eluded us but that we need.[9]

Scripture can be read again and again with profit. Of course this is true of other texts too. A classic text is one from which people over time continue to draw strength and insight. Though we seldom read any ordinary book more than once, we can engage with the Bible over a lifetime, because it embodies the revelation of God whom we worship. Classics remain relevant over the centuries and go on illuminating lives. They serve as means of our hearing God's voice today. They do not just convey information; they leave their mark on our lives. They do not go out of date.

Not only does the Bible speak out of the past, but it addresses the future as well. It speaks not only of a world long gone but also of a new world that is coming. Thus it ignites hope and creates significance. The Bible should not be thought of as a closed circle, because it is open to the future fulfillment of God's promises. This is why when we read it we do not just look back to original meanings but to God who indwells us and is leading us forward. The text may point us to where we are to be going, if we are listening to God's voice. The Bible opens up a new world and bids us come and inhabit it. It is a revelatory text.[10]

Imagine that we were to find the unfinished text of a Shakespearean play—four acts complete, the final act lost. What would we do? Surely we would ask experienced actors to immerse themselves in the four extant acts and then project where they think the play was heading. This is like the situation we face with the Bible. We have four acts complete and find ourselves having to actualize what they are pointing to. We have to be faithful to what is written, but we have also to be creative and open to where the Spirit is taking us. The context for this ongoing application of the Bible is the fellowship of the community that follows God as he leads us forth into greater redemption.

Meditating on Scripture

Because God's Word is dynamic and open, we need to learn to meditate on Scripture. Building on careful exegesis of the text, we strive to enter the subject matter more profoundly.

Take a narrative, a psalm, a promise, a warning—and let it become something personal for you. Let the text be a living word, let it take root. Receive the word into the soil of your heart, and ponder it as you wait on God and listen. You will be made clean by the word that is spoken to you, and you will become rooted, built up and established in faith (Col 2:7). God gives us the Bible not just for information but for transformation, for the reordering of our lives.[11]

Those who cannot read or readily grasp the ideas of the Bible have teachers to explain the Scriptures through commentary. Philip was sent into the desert to help the Ethiopian to understand the prophet Isaiah (Acts 8:26). Teachers feed the faith of others by mediating Scripture to them. Inevitably, teachers interpret the Bible according to a tradition, such as the Baptist or the Anglican. This reminds us that we are not dealing only with reader and text but also with community and tradition. This is inevitable and enriching, and also something to be aware of as we seek truth.

The parable of the sower explains how some hear the Word of God but do not allow it to germinate in them. Others receive it with great enthusiasm, but not deeply. For a while they believe, but in a time of testing they fall away. In others the anxieties of life and material pleasures hinder the Word from maturing. Jesus concludes by pointing to another possibility: "But as for that in the good soil, these are the ones who, when they hear the word, hold it fast in an honest and good heart, and bear fruit with patient endurance" (Lk 8:15).

People around the world are nourished by the Bible because of translation. In hundreds of languages and cultures throughout the world, the Bible has brought churches into being and nourished them in the faith. It is not cultural imperialism to want to see the Bible in every language, because the gospel offers humanity a possibility for existence that ought to be known and available to them. It is a message people have the right to decide about. To withhold the Bible from them would restrict their choice and prevent them being able to consider the truth that has liberated us. Money and fame are not the motivation for Bible translation, but a passion for the truth that sets us free.

Churches exist among illiterate peoples, and in these circumstances the Bible is read aloud, expressed in liturgy and explained by preaching. Even in literate settings, spiritual life is maintained as we feed on the Bible indirectly through hymns, prayers, readings and proclamation in the local church.

Bible and Community

Christianity is marked by a new fellowship, and the Bible is central to maintaining this. It enables people to enter the conversation of the triune God with the people of God. The Bible makes the conversation happen. It gives us the language for conversing with God. We come to it with our hopes and fears, wanting to be nourished and renewed. We bring our questions, we argue, and we find ourselves being changed. We know it to be the inspired Word of God because of its effect on us.

It affects us as individuals as we feed upon it in times of quiet. We also hear the Word read aloud in the community. The lectionary gives us a balanced diet of readings, exposing us to biography, proverb, narrative, prayer, instruction and parable. All of these forms function in various ways to speak to us and to engage our lives as worshipers.

The community also receives the biblical metaphors indirectly through hymns and liturgy, preaching and prayers, bodily gestures and dance. Children are nourished from their earliest days on simpler versions of the biblical metaphors and stories in their education classes. Young believers may come to the Bible with diverse components of various faith models. As the Word speaks, they begin to sort things out and discard what no longer works for them. Questions are addressed to the Bible, which in turn gives them new insight, and the model is refined and tried in real-life situations. Reflection on Scripture is never finished—reformation and renewal need to continue always.

It is important to grow as hearers of the Word of God, to get beyond looking to the Bible as a magical book of answers and to see it as the Spirit's witness to the love of God revealed in Jesus Christ. We must open ourselves to the whole Bible in all its variety and listen to it not only as individuals but also in community, allowing ourselves to be shaped by what others find. We have to be bold enough to take responsibility for fresh readings and applications in the present setting and allow ourselves to be transformed in the direction of greater love for God and one another.

The Bible is not always easy to interpret. We used the Bible to justify keeping slaves in the eighteenth and nineteenth centuries! Some are taking a similar tack now by using the Bible to try to keep women in their place. Others, in reaction, reject the Bible outright because they think it requires a patriarchal God and dominating husbands.

We think the problem can be solved with a little effort at fresh exegesis. If Paul could have asked slaves to submit to their masters without supporting slavery (as all agree he did), could he not have asked wives to submit to their husbands without supporting male dominance over women?[12] We come to the Bible with our questions and, by struggling with the text, find directions of hope and love to guide us.[13]

Shifting Models

Christians have to test the models they use for understanding aspects of biblical revelation. Even if we are equally committed to the Bible as the Word of God, we may differ sometimes as to what model to adopt. Denominations derive different models from Scripture. Because of the text's complexity, it is hard to read the Bible without any model whatsoever. But models can be compared and allowed to interact with one another. One model can be set over against another to see which is most helpful.

We experience a shift of model when someone presents us with metaphors that are different from the ones we are used to. The challenge may come not in an intellectual form but in unsuspected ways. For example, music may convey a new understanding. New songs may herald a change of model. The Methodists produced a whole new set of hymns that carried the freight of the evangelical revival in an affective form. In our day the songs of the charismatic renewal and the work of songwriters like Graham Kendrick signal theological and spiritual change. The exuberance of praise encouraged by such songs is in obvious contrast with restrained traditional worship. The older forms were rich in content but weak in spontaneity. The new music challenges the notion that the church ought to consist of one big mouth and a lot of little ears. There are cultural factors at work, of course, but a new model is also at work, directing us to the loving heart of God and setting us free.

The Bible provides the raw material for constructing models and correcting them when needed. The Bible is infallible; our models and interpretations are not. When others contest our model, we do not conclude that they are heretics. Not everyone will reach exactly the same conclusions as ours. If they embrace another model, it does not follow that they are unspiritual. We are all fallible interpreters. We welcome differing opinions, not as relativists but because truth is the goal of our striving and it is not arrived at quickly and easily.

We find the Bible teaching a model of creative love, but we recognize the right of others to develop and pursue other models. We are interested in them as possibly valid ways for understanding revelation. It is enriching to explore different models for interpreting the Bible and to learn from them whatever we can.

We are committed to a particular model by which we live, but we are also open to change. Ours is a pilgrim, not a fortress, theology. Our theology is a path of discovery. When we make mistakes, we return to the main path and begin again. We may be able to understand a metaphor in a new way or find a larger model that is more elegant and compelling than our present one. In this book we recommend that people live and order their lives by the model of creative love theism in the confidence that the Spirit will guide us into any further truth.

XVI
FELLOWSHIP
Enjoying
Love

IN THE APOSTLES' CREED WE DECLARE OUR FAITH IN THE COMMUNION OF saints, and in a blessing Paul commends us to a participation in the Holy Spirit (2 Cor 13:13). This language refers to what we share as partakers of God's Spirit and to the community of brothers and sisters that we have become.

In the world there are those who lord it over others and jealously guard their possessions. Jesus speaks against this: "It will not be so among you, but whoever wishes to be great among you must be your servant, and whoever wishes to be first among you must be your slave; just as the Son of Man came not to be served but to serve, and to give his life a ransom for many" (Mt 20:26-28). His words were heard and took form in the early church when believers sold their goods and gave to any in need (Acts 2:44-46). The lust for power and idolatry of possessions were being broken, the privileges of race, class and gender were beginning to break down. Christians were beginning to experience a new oneness in Jesus Christ (Gal 3:28). They were becoming a society of friends who welcomed one another with affection and treated the despised with respect.[1]

A Society of Friends

The experience of open friendship is an important sacrament for encountering God's love. Our fellowship in Christ is a means of grace. Having experienced the love of God, we participate in the fellowship of the Spirit in the community of the new creation. We are being joined to an open, inviting fellowship mirroring the Trinity; every creature is summoned to find a place here.[2] This speaks to the longing of the current generation, which searches for community and yearns to become whole.[3] God first engenders love in us, binding us to him and freeing us to be ourselves, and then invites us to grow, not in isolation but in community.

God gives himself to us in order to create this new community. He draws us without coercion into relationships. In this new community, marked by mutuality and reciprocity, we become free to open ourselves to one another and share our lives. Any society is normally open to people who share class and culture; our community is unique in not existing only for people like ourselves. Membership is thrown open to all sorts of people.

The image of God in us is social—male and female together reflect the social nature of the triune God. The Christian fellowship constitutes a restoration of God's image in us.[4] It restores the purpose of our existence as social beings and anticipates life in communion with God beyond death. Eternal life will consist in oneness with others and with the triune God. The goal of redemption is not private salvation in isolation but redeemed society in which love flows through personal relationships. We look for a community without threat or discrimination, without fear or hatred. The image of God in us is being restored as we fellowship with God and with others. By the grace of God we are being restored to the family.

Relationships should not be an unpleasant duty that we attend to unwillingly. Recluses are hiding from life, and they need to be opened up and healed. Participation in the Spirit should cause us increasingly to welcome opportunities to participate in community—to contribute and pray, to sing and worship—in anticipation of the coming world.

Jesus was a friend of tax collectors and sinners (Lk 7:34); he treated them with affection and respect for who they were and what they could become. Jesus says that we are God's friends and must be friends to one another (Jn 15:12-15). We belong to a new community of friends where everyone is welcome. It is not a closed circle or a group limited to persons like ourselves. The circle is open. As God's friends, we must be friends to everyone in the spirit of the kingdom Jesus announced.

Fellowship is not merely an affair of the heart; it involves both body and soul. We express our love for one another in words and in bodily ways—when we kiss and embrace, pray and lay on hands, pass the peace and share in the Eucharistic meal. We weep with those that weep and rejoice with those who rejoice (Rom 12:15). Fellowship encompasses the whole of our life and engages the senses. Bodily acts proclaim that we love one another and value the relationship. Love has its ways of looking and acting. The kindly touch, the loving embrace, the compassionate glance are powerful gestures that convey more than can be put into words.[5]

Since there are five references to the kiss of peace in the New Testament, evidently this was an accepted practice in the early church, as it is today in the Near East and elsewhere. The holy kiss or hug expresses acceptance, forgiveness and community among believers. It is a concrete sign of fellowship and community. It is ironic that the very people who are literal-minded and unyielding on other biblical commandments can simply ignore five unqualified commands without sensing the inconsistency.

Kinship Groups

Churches need to foster deeper fellowship. Depth in relationships is essential for the church to be the church and for the body to minister in the power of the Spirit so that all its parts work in harmony. Shallow friendships make churches ineffective as vehicles of God's mission. A small group structure is needed to foster fellowship and deepen friendships.

Small groups, where deep levels of sharing can occur, have always been a mark of vital churches.[6] Relationships in church must go far beyond the hello and goodby of Sunday morning. Small groups have much to contribute by way of pastoral care, identifying gifts, bearing burdens and holding people accountable. John Wesley thought people who did not belong to a discipleship group were not serious about being Christian.[7]

Many churches focus on low-commitment rather than high-commitment meetings. In addition to the weekly celebration, there need to be friendship groups for in-depth fellowship, equipping for ministry and caring support. There needs to be a network of small groups within the larger church where people can share what God is doing in their lives and relate lovingly with one another.[8]

Small groups provide many strengths to the larger body. Because the group is small, it can be flexible in adapting to changing circumstances. It is mobile and can meet where people are. It is inclusive and often nonhierarchical. It has no budget, no officers, nothing to promote except relationships. It is personal. It can reach people presently untouched by the church and complement what the larger body is doing. Seekers can easily enter the church through the small group. There is no structure more effective at communicating the gospel than a small group of believers meeting informally in their homes.

A church is necessarily an institution. It has a street address, a phone number, regular assemblies and a constitution. But the purpose of the institution is to nurture community and promote mission. As the flowerpot exists for the plant, so the institution exists for community to flourish, and from community, in turn, mission flows to the world.

Acceptance and Transformation

Fellowship refers to sharing the grace of God and is also a term for those who accept one another. We are forgiven people who have begun a process of being changed into Christ's likeness. We are not here because we are good people—those outside church may be nobler than we are. Much in us still needs changing, but God is not finished with us yet.

Fellowship is more than acceptance. Members of many groups have high tolerance for each other's faults. Acceptance is an important start, but fellowship also aims at transformation. Since we are being changed into God's likeness, we look at each other in the light of what we will become.

Alcoholics on skid row accept one other—but they do so without expectation of change for the better. Things will only get worse until death ends the stupor. But we hope for transformation and new creation.

We are looking for a process of change by the Spirit. We trust God for this and must not try to take it over. If we manipulate persons into doing what we think is good for them, they will resist. They will not trust those who interfere. We leave God to do the changing in his own way, according to his own sequence. We do not know how to get at people's problems. We do not know the priority of corrections needed. We may think a certain fault is glaring when something deeper is the underlying problem.

In the 1950s J. B. Phillips wrote a book called *Your God Is Too Small.* Maybe we now need a book called *Your God Is Too Fast!* Too readily we try to make God operate according to our rushed schedules. In both creation and redemption God takes a lot of time. God does not seem to be a hurry. He knows how to work in a person's life and how to pace it. A thousand years of our time is just a day for God. God goes by his own schedule.

It doesn't help when we nag people about what's wrong with them and what they should be doing next. Such interference is likely to cause resentment and do more harm than good. Faith trusts God to work holiness in his own way and in the appropriate sequence.[9]

We do not often see Jesus correcting the bad habits of the disciples. He had strong words for legalists, and the epistles severely reprove false teachers, but there is mostly positive encouragement for people to exercise their priesthood. There is no nagging interference in people's lives.

This does not imply an attitude of indifference. Concern about the faults of others should be brought to God in prayer, not to them. We talk to God about the behavior that upsets us and ask the Spirit to work in the other person's life. As we go deeper in prayer conversation with God, we may catch glimpses of the hurt, abuse and deprivation that are causing the damage. The process of change can be facilitated without abusing one another's self-respect. In prayer we hand each other over to God to be changed by him. Such prayer is an expression of our faith, and it is the most loving thing we can do.

Prayer gives loving support unobtrusively. It is the strong foundation of vital fellowship. In prayer we yield to God to do the renewing work.

Accepting Our Acceptance

The failure of Christian growth can have serious consequences but does not put salvation in jeopardy. When we are baptized into the fellowship, God assures us we are forgiven, and we should assure others too. God knows our frailty and forgives us. He does not keep an account of our sins. Although we know God forgives sins, often our hardest challenge is not forgiving others but forgiving ourselves.

Community helps us cope with this difficulty. Here we are given the assurance that we are loved and accepted, however much we fail. It is hard for us to believe in divine forgiveness unless our fellows accept us unconditionally too. When the local church expresses acceptance in its life and worship, God's love is powerfully sensed, faith is increased, and new people are drawn to Christ.

In the fellowship we are accepted and forgiven, whatever our faults. And since we have been shown such mercy, we must take care not to reject the love of God for others. If there is someone we refuse to accept, the fellowship is broken and the assurance of our own forgiveness is called in question. The Lord's Prayer reminds us of this: "Forgive us our debts, as we also have forgiven our debtors." Later Jesus adds, "If you forgive others their trespasses, your heavenly Father will also forgive you; but if you do not forgive others, neither will your Father forgive your trespasses" (Mt 6:12, 14-15). God does not reject us for refusing to forgive, but our refusing to forgive has serious consequences.

When we start thinking others owe us an apology and need to prove they are sorry and will perform better in future, we may be refusing to forgive a trespass. Refusal to forgive is a sickness in us. What right do we have to enjoy unmerited forgiveness if we do not extend it to others? The forgiven but unforgiving servant in the parable finds himself in deep trouble (Mt 18:21-35).

If we forgive readily, does this mean license? No, because people reap what they sow by their actions (Gal 6:7). God's wrath assigns consequences to our actions even while he loves and forgives us. God feels the pain of self-destructive behavior and assigns consequences. We too need to assign consequences for behavior.

If someone helps herself to money out of the offering plate, we can make sure the plate is empty when it is passed to her next time. This does not contradict our continuing to love and forgive her as God does.

If someone makes inappropriate sexual advances, consequences should be assigned and precautions taken. A single woman would not want to accompany this person to his apartment alone. But the person can still be loved and forgiven and can learn through this difficulty what love means.

Loving intimacy between men and women in church need not lead to immorality. Having tasted what genuine love is, we learn to view others not as objects of desire but as persons—every woman a sister and every man a brother.

Risky Business
Acceptance is risky business. Jesus' policy of open friendship led him to invite to God's banquet anyone who might choose to come. His was an accepting lifestyle that welcomed all and sundry into fellowship. The church is a school of the Spirit. A school takes in pupils who are ignorant and undisciplined at first.

But a school cannot survive long unless its teachers are reliable. The same Jesus who welcomed sinners to his circle also denounced the teachers of the law. A school for sinners needs teachers who know what is going on and who are in line with God's way of acceptance and transformation. One must distinguish between strong measures for dealing with false teachers and the gentle treatment of ordinary disciples.

There is also a fine line between a student who is behaving badly and one who sets out to disrupt. Unruly students cannot be permitted to undermine the purpose for which the school exists. In a school, if a boy comes to class, lights up a joint and begins to sell drugs during class, even the most accepting teacher must send the student to the principal. On one occasion Paul had to exclude a man from the congregation on account of flagrant sexual sins, but even then Paul's stated goal was restoration (1 Cor 5:1-5; 2 Cor 2:5-11).

The Body of Christ

The church is pictured as a body with different members and limbs. Belonging to church means having a function in the community. There are lists of these functions in the New Testament, lists of the kinds of things members might find themselves doing. The Spirit apportions a variety of gifts among those who are ready to function. It is important for us to welcome the full variety of gifts and release their potential.

The Spirit has quickened and gifted us all, each in his or her own way. We all have our own charism from God. This is true even of the most unlikely. The disabled, for example, correspond to the crucified Christ. Everyone belongs here, and there is room for all—strong and weak, rich and poor, wise and foolish.

Among the endowments there are everyday gifts of ordinary life as well as more unusual gifts. There are gifts of proclamation by male and female witnesses, gifts of service and ministry, gifts of healing and miracles that confront the dark powers and restore brokenness. There are all sorts of gifts for use in ministry.

Some persons have the apostolic gift for establishing new churches, others can pray in unknown tongues, others confront the powers of death in healing prayer. No strict distinctions can be drawn between the functions of evangelistic preaching, church teaching, pastoral work and prophetic ministry. Faith may be expressed in gifts of serving, in music, in showing mercy, in praying and caring for the sick. These are all different ways in which the Spirit is manifested in the community.

The gift of speaking in other tongues is valuable, though often misunderstood. Its exercise easily gives rise to charges of drunkenness and madness (Acts 2:13; 1 Cor 14:23). But Paul values it as a type of prayer. He makes a distinction between conscious mental prayer and the intuitive prayer of the spirit. He says that one can pray and sing with both mind and spirit (1 Cor 14:15). We might say one can pray from the left or the right side of the brain. Tongues happen when ordinary speech will not suffice to express what the Spirit is prompting, as when pain can only be expressed by uncontrolled weeping and joy by jumping and dancing. Resistance to this gift may testify to the limitations and lack of spontaneity of our normal forms of expression in church.

Let the tongues of the dumb be loosed—let them express what they feel. Let there be room for the expression of every kind of gift and personality in our churches. Every person should be recognized as important and encouraged to make a contribution. Let none be unemployed in church.

Servant Leadership

Church ministry ought to be inclusive, not exclusive. No group should be excluded from exercising it. All are equally saved and called, and all races, classes, nationalities and genders are needed in the ministry of the church.

A congregation is weakened when a single person is ordained to order its life and the members do little more than assist this ordained person. Such a one (if hardworking) can generate a certain amount of activity. But how limited in fruitfulness are his or her efforts in comparison to the ministry of the whole body! A "one-person show" forces those who could be exercising gifts in the community to be passive. A capable minister may be able to engage in varied activity, but everyone is programmed to dance to his or her tune. We need to trust the Spirit to work through everyone and not leave ministry to a single person.

The word *ministry* originally meant quite menial service, but eventually it came to denote authority over, order, control. Yet Jesus was among us as one who served. Ministry means servanthood. The purpose of leadership is to equip saints for ministry. Thinking of ministry in terms of nurturing the gifts of others requires faith in the Spirit and his gifts. It also means accepting the risk of mistakes, unanticipated events and dubious manifestations of gifts of the Spirit.

God's concern about fellowship goes beyond the church. He cares about the whole world, for the church is a foretaste of a new humanity. God is concerned about the kingdom, not just the church. Therefore God delights in and fosters fellowship everywhere on every level, inside churches and outside them. God loves to make life worth living and cares about healing and reconciling people. God loves community in every form. He cares about communities in creation as well as redemption.

Practically everything is a complex of particles, the whole much greater than the sum of its parts. Creation manifests a wealth of patterns and forms. The Spirit of life creates communities everywhere—families, marriages, natural and voluntary communities, action groups, self-help groups, friendships of every kind. God calls us together and is moving us toward reconciliation and resurrection.

Conclusion

"The thief comes only to steal and kill and destroy. I came that they may have life, and have it abundantly"—these are the words of Jesus to all persons (Jn 10:10). Jesus understood the hesitancy of the woman at the well as her not knowing the gift of God, how great and extensive it was (Jn 4:10). This is good news theology; it is the megashift we have needed: God is a Father who cares for us, not a judge criticizing from a distance.

But how common it is for people inside and outside the church not to know the full extent of God's grace. They will image God as a cosmic moralist or an impersonal absolute or an all-controlling power, and not recognize him as the Father and Lover who calls us all to come and embrace him. We need to focus anew on the grace and love of God.

Listen to the Song of Solomon:
My beloved speaks and says to me:
"Arise, my love, my fair one,
    and come away;
for now the winter is past,
    the rain is over and gone. . . .
Arise, my love, my fair one,
    and come away.
O my dove, in the clefts of the rock,
    in the covert of the cliff,
let me see your face,
    let me hear your voice;
for your voice is sweet,

and your face is lovely. . . .

My beloved is mine and I am his;

he pastures his flock among the lilies. (Song 2:10-11, 13-14, 16)

Our Lover is calling to us. Let us embrace God's sublime beauty and radiance. Let God's beauty awaken your desire and flood your being with love. At his right hand are pleasures forevermore (Ps 16:11).

Augustine laments his tardiness to love:

Too late did I love thee, O Fairness, so ancient and yet so new. Too late did I love thee. For behold, thou wert within, and I without, and there did I seek thee. I, unlovely, rushed heedlessly among the things of beauty thou madest. Thou wert with me, but I was not with thee. Thou didst call and cry aloud, and forced open my deafness. Thou didst gleam and shine, and chase away my blindness. Thou didst exhale odors, and I drew in my breath and do pant after thee. I tasted and do hunger and thirst. Thou didst touch me and I burned for thy peace. (*Confessions* 10. 27)

God is so radiant that he deserves beautiful theology, theology done with joy and thankfulness, theology that can dance and sing. Karl Barth wrote: "Sulky faces, morose thoughts and boring ways of speaking are intolerable in this science."[1] Intolerable too are dark thoughts about God, in whom there is no darkness at all.

In our book we have sought to portray a vision of God, the dimensions of whose love are boundless and whom to know is life eternal. This is surely the best apologetic for faith. Proofs of God's existence, evidences for Christ's resurrection, explanations of difficult sayings—whatever value they may have, nothing can surpass the compelling power of a vision of God's grace. We want to lift up the grace, openness and reciprocity of God.

Our creation was a gift, and when evil entered in, grace abounded even more (Rom 5:20). God reconciled the world and has given everything a new future. A process of healing and reconciliation is under way and will issue in transformation and consummation.[2] It is not an easy process. It was easier for God to create the world than to redeem it now that it is broken. What an art to retrieve clay that was spoiled and reshape it into something lovely! But the power of God makes life new, the alchemy of his grace creates beauty out of ashes.

Receive God's love. Let him multiply the loaves and fishes of your life—let him take the little that you have and bless it. The prodigal squandered his own family's resources and betrayed its trust, but the father still welcomed him home without condemnation. He was not interested in discussing the reasons for the young man's bad behavior. The father was so overjoyed to see his son that he ran out to meet him, wrapping him in an embrace.

God is speaking to all of us: Whatever you have done, come home, just as you are. Do not dress up, do not try to appear worthy. I receive and forgive you—my grace will transform and change you.

We celebrate the mystery of God's love and acceptance. The power that brought the world into being is working to bring out the potential of every creature. God's salvation makes it possible to realize our potential in partnership with God. Our creation in God's image was the beginning of the process that comes to fruition when we respond to the offer of God's gracious presence.

God's grace is with us, calling us out of self-centeredness into a life of love, sustaining us in our halting efforts to serve God, granting us the gift of God's self-communication. Grace is a gift that reaches its goal when it is received by the human person. Grace makes the response possible but does not negate the need of responding.

Our purpose here is to lift up the transforming ways of God with us. God is gracious in offering us a transforming friendship. No other religion has this to offer, no other model in theology highlights it so well.

Love divine, all loves excelling,
Joy of heaven to earth come down;
Fix in us thy humble dwelling,
All thy faithful mercies crown.
Jesus, thou art all compassion,
Pure, unbounded love thou art;
Visit us with thy salvation,
Enter every trembling heart.

Breathe, O breathe thy loving Spirit
Into every troubled breast!
Let us all in thee inherit,
Let us find that promised rest.
Take away our bent to sinning,
Alpha and Omega be;
End of faith, as its beginning,

Set our hearts at liberty.

Come, Almighty, to deliver,
Let us all thy life receive;
Suddenly return and never,
Nevermore thy temples leave.
Thee we would be always blessing,
Serve thee as thy hosts above,
Pray and praise thee without ceasing,
Glory in thy perfect love.

Finish then thy new creation,
Pure and spotless let us be;
Let us see thy great salvation
Perfectly restored in thee;
Changed from glory into glory,
Till in heaven we take our place,
Till we cast our crowns before thee,
Lost in wonder, love and praise.
(Charles Wesley)

NOTES

Introduction

[1]On theology as an ongoing exercise see Michael Bauman, *Pilgrim Theology: Taking the Path of Theological Discovery* (Grand Rapids, Mich.: Zondervan, 1992).

[2]These books include *Religion, Origins and Ideas* (Chicago: InterVarsity Press, 1966), *The Church: An Organic Picture* (Grand Rapids, Mich.: Eerdmans, 1968) and *Go Make Learners: A Discipleship Model of the Church* (Wheaton, Ill.: Harold Shaw, 1982).

[3]Pinnock's books include *The Scripture Principle* (San Francisco: Harper & Row, 1984), *Tracking the Maze* (San Francisco: Harper & Row, 1990) and *A Wideness in God's Mercy* (Grand Rapids, Mich.: Zondervan, 1992).

[4]Though our book does not often press this key, we see similarities with feminist theology when it is done in a classical way, as for example by Elizabeth A. Johnson, *She Who Is: The Mystery of God in Feminist Theological Discourse* (New York: Crossroad, 1992).

[5]To address this problem, Pinnock earlier edited *The Grace of God, the Will of Man: A Case for Arminianism* (Grand Rapids, Mich.: Zondervan, 1989), which was in its own way a statement of creative love theism.

[6]Another book from InterVarsity Press, *The Openness of God* (1994), written by Clark Pinnock, Richard Rice, John Sanders, William Hasker and David Basinger, deals with the openness of God. It seeks to retrieve this biblical idea from long-standing neglect but puts less stress on the legal distortion that is central to Brow's original concern.

[7]We think of simple books for the general reader which disregard tough issues even though they are written by very competent authors; examples include J. I. Packer, *Concise Theology* (Wheaton, Ill.: Tyndale House, 1993), and Charles C. Ryrie, *Basic Theology* (Wheaton, Ill.: Victor Books, 1986). No doubt these books serve a purpose, but we really need more mature statements from such theologians.

[8]There are evangelical theologians who take time to do quality work, such as Millard Erickson, *Christian Theology*, 3 vols. (Grand Rapids, Mich.: Baker Book House, 1983-85), and Gordon R. Lewis and Bruce A. Demarest, *Integrative Theology* (Grand Rapids, Mich.: Zondervan, 1991). But even they do not take many risks to explore fresh thinking.

[9]We welcome with enthusiasm Stanley J. Grenz, *Revisioning Evangelical Theology: A Fresh Agenda for the 21st Century* (Downers Grove, Ill.: InterVarsity Press, 1993), as the sort of creative work that may win a hearing for our faith in the modern

situation. We also delight in the tone of Richard Lints, *The Fabric of Theology: A Prolegomena to Evangelical Theology* (Grand Rapids, Mich.: Eerdmans, 1993).

[10]One who may see it this way is Robert A. Morey, *Battle of the Gods: The Gathering Storm in Modern Evangelicalism* (Southbridge, Mass.: Crown, 1989).

[11]On the link between Paul and Jesus, see Ralph P. Martin, *Reconciliation: A Study of Paul's Theology* (Atlanta: John Knox, 1981).

[12]This point gives the doctrine of justification by faith a more personal meaning by placing it in the family context, not just in the courtroom. See Thomas C. Oden, *Life in the Spirit* (San Francisco: HarperSanFrancisco, 1992), pp. 127-28, 255-56.

[13]A systematic theology that grasps our model well is Daniel L. Migliore, *Faith Seeking Understanding: An Introduction to Christian Theololgy* (Grand Rapids, Mich.: Eerdmans, 1991).

Chapter 1: Religion: Models of Love

[1]David A. Rausch and Carl H. Voss, *World Religions: Our Quest for Meaning* (Valley Forge, Penn.: Trinity Press International, 1993). Pinnock also calls for interreligious dialogue in *A Wideness in God's Mercy: The Finality of Jesus Christ in a World of Religions* (Grand Rapids, Mich.: Zondervan, 1992), chap. 4.

[2]See John A. DiNoia, *The Diversity of Religions: A Christian Perspective* (Washington, D.C.: Catholic University of America Press, 1992).

[3]Harold A. Netland sorts out the conflicting truth claims of the major religions by means of four questions in *Dissonant Voices: Religious Pluralism and the Question of Truth* (Grand Rapids, Mich.: Eerdmans, 1991), chaps. 2-3.

[4]Norman L. Geisler presents the various forms of naturalism in *Is Man the Measure? An Evaluation of Contemporary Humanism* (Grand Rapids, Mich.: Baker Book House, 1983).

[5]On the primitive religions, see John P. Newport, *Life's Ultimate Questions* (Waco, Tex.: Word, 1989), chap. 9.

[6]John B. Noss, *Man's Religions* (New York: Macmillan, 1969), pt. 3.

[7]See Michael Carrithers, *The Buddha* (New York: Oxford University Press, 1983).

[8]On monism, see Norman L. Geisler and William D. Watkins, *Perspectives: Understanding and Evaluating Today's World Views* (San Bernardino, Calif.: Here's Life, 1984), chap. 4.

Chapter 2: Theism: Creative Love

[1]On the meaning of creation, see Langdon Gilkey, *Maker of Heaven and Earth: The Christian Doctrine of Creation in the Light of Modern Knowledge* (New York: Doubleday, 1959).

[2]Charles E. Hummel, *The Galileo Connection: Resolving Conflicts Between Science and the Bible* (Downers Grove, Ill.: InterVarsity Press, 1986), chap. 12.

[3]Conrad Hyers, *The Meaning of Creation: Genesis and Modern Science* (Atlanta: John Knox, 1984).

[4]See Anne Cooper, *Ishmael, My Brother: A Christian Introduction to Islam* (Tunbridge Wells, Kent: MARC, 1985), and Norman Geisler and Abdul Saleeb, *Answering Islam: The Crescent in the Light of the Cross* (Grand Rapids, Mich.: Baker Book House, 1993).

[5]For further reflections on Islam, see Kenneth Cragg, *The Call of the Minaret* (Maryknoll, N.Y.: Orbis Books, 1985).

⁶See Stephen Westerholm, *Israel's Law and the Church's Faith* (Grand Rapids, Mich.: Eerdmans, 1988).

⁷Holmes Ralston does not pin the blame on Calvin himself so much as on later developments: *John Calvin Versus the Westminster Confession* (Richmond, Va.: John Knox, 1972).

⁸See B. B. Warfield's discussion of old Catholicism in *The Plan of Salvation* (Grand Rapids, Mich.: Eerdmans, 1955), chap. 3.

⁹On the faith principle, see John Sanders, *No Other Name: An Investigation into the Destiny of the Unevangelized* (Grand Rapids, Mich.: Eerdmans, 1992), pp. 224-32.

¹⁰Hans Küng, *Christianity and the World Religions: Paths to Dialogue with Islam, Hinduism and Buddhism* (New York: Doubleday, 1986).

¹¹For help with finding our way to God, see Thomas V. Morris, *Making Sense of It All: Pascal and the Meaning of Life* (Grand Rapids, Mich.: Eerdmans, 1992).

Chapter 3: Resurrection: Victorious Love

¹For an introduction to the category of resurrection, see George Eldon Ladd, *I Believe in the Resurrection of Jesus* (Grand Rapids, Mich.: Eerdmans, 1975).

²On such issues of history and philosophy, see Stephen T. Davis, *Risen Indeed: Making Sense of the Resurrection* (Grand Rapids, Mich.: Eerdmans, 1993).

³For theology of the resurrection, see Walter Kunneth, *The Theology of the Resurrection* (St. Louis: Concordia, 1965), pts. 2-3.

⁴A most capable study of resurrection is by Murray J. Harris, *Raised Immortal: Resurrection and Immortality in the New Testament* (Grand Rapids, Mich.: Eerdmans, 1983).

⁵On the resurrection as hope, see Jürgen Moltmann, *Theology of Hope* (New York: Harper & Row, 1967).

⁶Richard B. Gaffin notes this in *Resurrection and Redemption: A Study in Paul's Soteriology* (Grand Rapids, Mich.: Baker Book House, 1978).

⁷On the resurrection as theodicy, see John Hick, *Death and Eternal Life* (London: Collins, 1976), chap. 8.

⁸C. S. Lewis, *Mere Christianity* (London: Fontana, 1952), p. 116.

⁹John W. Cooper, *Body, Soul and Life Everlasting: Biblical Anthropology and the Monism-Dualism Debate* (Grand Rapids, Mich.: Eerdmans, 1989).

¹⁰On the replica theory of resurrection, see Hick, *Death and Eternal Life*, chap. 15.

Chapter 4: Trinity: Personal Love

¹For some introduction, see Alister E. McGrath, *Understanding the Trinity* (Grand Rapids, Mich.: Zondervan, 1988).

²Leonard Hodgson assisted in the recovery of this truth: *The Doctrine of the Trinity* (London: Nisbet, 1943). Also, Arthur W. Wainwright, *The Trinity in the New Testament* (London: SPCK, 1962).

³Jürgen Moltmann lifts this truth up in *The Trinity and the Kingdom* (San Francisco: Harper & Row, 1981).

⁴Daniel L. Migliore, *Faith Seeking Understanding: An Introduction to Christian Theology* (Grand Rapids, Mich.: Eerdmans, 1991), p. 63.

⁵This is brought out by Cornelius Plantinga, "The Perfect Family," *Christianity Today*, March 4, 1988, and by Catherine M. LaCugna, "The Practical Trinity," *Christian Century*, July 15, 1992.

[6]For a full discussion of the doctrine of the Spirit, see Jürgen Moltmann, *The Spirit of Life: A Universal Affirmation* (Minneapolis: Fortress, 1992).

Chapter 5: Diagnosis: Defective Love

[1]Langdon Gilkey explains how he came to realize how deep the problem of sin runs in *Shantung Compound: The Story of Men and Women Under Pressure* (New York: Harper & Row, 1966).

[2]Systematic theologies often fail to identify the essence of sin, preferring just to record the multiplicity of biblical terms for it; see Millard Erickson, *Christian Theology* (Grand Rapids, Mich.: Baker Book House, 1984), pt. 6. There is value in trying to get to the heart of the matter.

[3]On the the image of God, see Philip E. Hughes, *The True Image: The Origin and Destiny of Man in Christ* (Grand Rapids, Mich.: Eerdmans, 1989).

[4]Karl Menninger, *Whatever Became of Sin?* (New York: Hawthorn Books, 1973).

[5]Gregory A. Boyd has helpful thoughts in *Trinity and Process: A Critical Evaluation and Reconstruction of Hartshorne's Di-polar Theism Towards a Trinitarian Metaphysics* (New York: Peter Lang, 1992), pp. 396-99.

[6]Harry R. Boer, *An Ember Still Glowing: Humankind as the Image of God* (Grand Rapids, Mich.: Eerdmans, 1990).

[7]Clark H. Pinnock, *A Wideness in God's Mercy: The Finality of Jesus Christ in a World of Religion* (Grand Rapids, Mich.: Zondervan, 1992), chap. 3.

[8]On Western views of original sin, see John Murray, *The Imputation of Adam's Sin* (Grand Rapids, Mich.: Eerdmans, 1959).

[9]George Vandervelde, *Original Sin: Two Major Trends in Contemporary Roman Catholic Reinterpretation* (Washington, D.C.: University Press of America, 1981).

[10]For a comparison between original sin in Augustine and in Irenaeus, see John Hick, *Evil and the God of Love* (New York: Harper & Row, 1966).

Chapter 6: Judgment: Caring Love

[1]Paul K. Jewett, *God, Creation and Revelation: A Neo-evangelical Theology* (Grand Rapids, Mich.: Eerdmans, 1991), p. 246.

[2]So Abraham J. Heschel, *The Prophets* (New York: Harper & Row, 1962), chap. 16.

[3]George B. Caird, *A Commentary on the Revelation of St. John the Divine* (London: Adam and Charles Black, 1966), p. 300.

[4]Ralph P. Martin, *Reconciliation: A Study of Paul's Theology* (Atlanta: John Knox, 1981), pp. 32-37.

Chapter 7: Advent: Active Love

[1]Best known among such works is Jürgen Moltmann, *Theology of Hope* (New York: Harper & Row, 1967). See also Thomas Finger, *Christian Theology: An Eschatological Approach,* vols. 1-2 (Scottdale, Penn.: Herald, 1989).

[2]On the doctrine of hope, see Stephen Travis, *I Believe in the Second Coming of Christ* (Grand Rapids, Mich.: Eerdmans, 1982).

[3]Dale Moody, *The Hope of Glory* (Grand Rapids, Mich.: Eerdmans, 1964), and Anthony A. Hoekema, *The Bible and the Future* (Grand Rapids, Mich.: Eerdmans, 1979).

[4]G. R. Beasley-Murray, *Jesus and the Future* (London: Macmillan, 1954).

[5]N. T. Wright, *Who Was Jesus?* (Grand Rapids, Mich.: Eerdmans, 1992), pp. 54-58, and R. T. France, *Jesus and the Old Testament* (London: Inter-Varsity Press, 1971), pp. 227-39.

[6]George Weigel, *The Final Revolution: The Resistant Church and the Collapse of Communism* (New York: Oxford University Press, 1992).

Chapter 8: Hell: Rejecting Love

[1]John A. T. Robinson defends universal salvation: *In the End God: A Study of the Christian Doctrine of the Last Things* (London: James Clarke, 1950).

[2]A primer on hell and views of its nature is William Crockett, ed., *Four Views on Hell* (Grand Rapids, Mich.: Zondervan, 1992).

[3]C. S. Lewis takes this line in *The Problem of Pain* (London: Collins, 1957), pp. 106-16.

[4]So Anthony Flew, *God and Philosophy* (London: Hutchinson, 1966), pp. 56-57.

[5]C. S. Lewis, *The Great Divorce* (New York: Macmillan, 1946), and *The Problem of Pain* (London: Fontana, 1957), chap. 8.

[6]Stott defends this view in a dialogue with David Edwards: *Essentials: A Liberal-Evangelical Dialogue* (London: Hodder & Stoughton, 1988; published in the U.S. as *Evangelical Essentials* [Downers Grove, Ill.: InterVarsity Press, 1988]), pp. 312-20, while Daniel P. Fuller rejects it in *The Unity of the Bible* (Grand Rapids, Mich.: Zondervan, 1992), pp. 196-203.

[7]The best presentation is by Edward Fudge, *The Fire That Consumes* (Houston: Providential Press, 1982).

[8]E. G. Selwyn, *The First Epistle of St. Peter* (London: Macmillan, 1961), p. 358.

[9]Stott in *Essentials,* p. 314.

[10]John Sanders, *No Other Name: An Investigation into the Destiny of the Unevangelized* (Grand Rapids, Mich.: Eerdmans, 1992), chap. 7, and Clark H. Pinnock, *A Wideness in God's Mercy: The Finality of Jesus Christ in a World of Religion* (Grand Rapids, Mich.: Zondervan, 1992), chap. 5.

[11]Stephen T. Evans, *Risen Indeed: A Christian Philosophy of Resurrection* (Grand Rapids, Mich.: Eerdmans, 1993), pp. 159-65.

Chapter 9: Sacrifice: Unconditional Love

[1]See John R. W. Stott, *The Cross of Christ* (Downers Grove, Ill.: InterVarsity Press, 1986), and Colin E. Gunton, *The Actuality of Atonement* (Grand Rapids, Mich.: Eerdmans, 1989).

[2]Fisher Humphreys pursues this question in *The Death of Christ* (Nashville: Broadman, 1978).

[3]A helpful analysis of models is Gustaf Aulen, *Christus Victor* (Philadelphia: Muhlenberg, 1962).

[4]John Calvin *Institutes of the Christian Religion* 2. 15.

[5]Ralph P. Martin, *Reconciliation: A Study of Paul's Theology* (Atlanta: John Knox, 1981), pp. 87, 103, 151.

[6]Jürgen Moltmann, *The Way of Jesus Christ: Christology in Messianic Dimensions* (San Francisco: HarperSanFrancisco, 1990), pt. 4.

[7]Thomas Talbott, "What Jesus Did for Us," *The Reformed Journal,* March 1990, pp. 8-12.

[8]Vincent Brummer, "Atonement and Reconciliation," *Religious Studies* 28 (1992): 435-52.

[9]See Jürgen Moltmann, *The Church in the Power of the Spirit* (London: SCM Press, 1977), pp. 93-98.

[10]Vernon White, *Atonement and Incarnation: An Essay in Universalism and Particularity* (New York: Cambridge University Press, 1991).

[11]John V. Dahms, "Dying with Christ," *Journal of the Evangelical Theolological Society* 36 (1993): 15-23.

Chapter 10: Liberation: Freeing Love

[1]On the breadth of the term see Michael Green, *The Meaning of Salvation* (London: Hodder & Stoughton, 1965). On the variety of its meanings see David F. Wells, *The Search for Salvation* (Downers Grove, Ill.: InterVarsity Press, 1978).

[2]Barth treats salvation in this pattern in *Church Dogmatics*, pt. 4.

[3]Gayraud S. Wilmore and James H. Cone, editors, *Black Theology: A Documentary History, 1966-1979* (Maryknoll, N.Y.: Orbis Books, 1979).

[4]Gustavo Gutiérrez, *A Theology of Liberation: History, Politics and Salvation* (Maryknoll, N.Y.: Orbis Books, 1973).

[5]Amy L. Sherman, *Preferential Option: A Christian and Neoliberal Strategy for Latin America's Poor* (Grand Rapids, Mich.: Eerdmans, 1992).

[6]Paul R. Smith, *Is It OK to Call God "Mother"?* (Peabody, Mass.: Hendrickson, 1993).

[7]Delwin Brown and Clark H. Pinnock, *Theological Crossfire: An Evangelical-Liberal Dialogue* (Grand Rapids, Mich.: Zondervan, 1990), pt. 1 on theological method.

[8]One could have wished that Millard Erickson had not defined salvation so narrowly in this way in *Christian Theology*, p. 905.

[9]Peter Toon, *Justification and Sanctification* (Westchester, Ill.: Crossway Books, 1983).

[10]Jürgen Moltmann chooses freedom as the primary category for his doctrine of salvation in *The Spirit of Life: A Universal Affirmation* (Minneapolis: Fortress, 1992), chap. 5.

[11]Richard N. Longenecker discusses them in *New Testament Social Ethics for Today* (Grand Rapids, Mich.: Eerdmans, 1984).

Chapter 11: Baptism: Invitation Love

[1]George R. Beasley-Murray, *Baptism in the New Testament* (London: Macmillan, 1963).

[2]Joachim Jeremias, *Jesus' Promise to the Nations* (London: SCM Press, 1958).

[3]I. Howard Marshall, *Kept by the Power of God: A Study of Perseverance and Falling Away* (London: Epworth Press, 1969).

Chapter 12: Church: Window Love

[1]David Watson, *I Believe in the Church* (Grand Rapids, Mich.: Eerdmans, 1978), and Eric G. Jay, *The Church: Its Changing Image Through Twenty Centuries* (London: SPCK, 1978).

[2]Two impressive books on the church are Jürgen Moltmann, *The Church in the Power of the Spirit: A Contribution to Messianic Ecclesiology* (London: SCM Press, 1977), and Hans Küng, *The Church* (New York: Sheed and Ward, 1967).

[3]Howard A. Snyder, *The Community of the King* (Downers Grove, Ill.: InterVarsity Press, 1977).

[4]On church, mission and Pentecost, see Harry Boer, *Pentecost and Mission* (Grand Rapids, Mich.: Eerdmans, 1961).

[5]Paul S. Minear, *Images of the Church In the New Testament* (Philadelphia: Westminster Press, 1960), and Avery Dulles, *Models of the Church* (New York: Doubleday, 1974).

[6]Greg Ogden, *The New Reformation: Returning the Ministry to the People of God* (Grand Rapids, Mich.: Zondervan, 1990), and R. Paul Stevens, *Liberating the Laity: Equipping All the Saints for Ministry* (Downers Grove, Ill.: InterVarsity Press, 1985).

[7]Thomas C. Oden, *Pastoral Theology: Essentials of Ministry* (San Francisco: Harper & Row, 1983), chap. 4.

[8]Rex A. Koivisto, *One Lord, One Faith* (Wheaton, Ill.: Victor Books, 1993).

[9]John Frame issues a passionate cry for unity in *Evangelical Reunion: Denominations and the Body of Christ* (Grand Rapids, Mich.: Baker Book House, 1991).

Chapter 13: Prayer: Conversational Love

[1]Hans Küng has a fine exposition of the godly life as advancing God's cause, which is to advance the cause of a beloved humanity: *On Being a Christian* (London: Collins, 1977), pp. 214-77.

[2]James Houston, *The Transforming Friendship* (Oxford: Lion, 1989); Kenneth Leech, *Experiencing God: Theology as Spirituality* (San Francisco: Harper & Row, 1985); Eugene H. Peterson, *A Long Obedience in the Same Direction* (Downers Grove, Ill.: InterVarsity Press, 1980).

[3]Alan J. Roxburgh, *Reaching a New Generation: Strategies for Tomorrow's Church* (Downers Grove, Ill: InterVarsity Press, 1993), chap. 8.

[4]Richard J. Foster is a very helpful guide: *Celebration of Discipline* (New York: Harper & Row, 1978) and *Prayer: Finding the Heart's True Home* (San Francisco: HarperSanFrancisco, 1992).

[5]Andrew Murray, *The Believer's Secret of Waiting on God* (Minneapolis: Bethany House, 1986).

[6]An introduction to the literature of devotion is Richard J. Foster and James B. Smith, eds., *Devotional Classics: Selected Readings for Individuals and Groups* (San Francisco: HarperSanFrancisco, 1993).

[7]Charles E. Hummel, *Fire in the Fireplace: Charismatic Renewal in the Nineties* (Downers Grove, Ill.: InterVarsity Press, 1993).

[8]Jürgen Moltmann, *The Spirit of Life: A Universal Affirmation* (Minneapolis: Fortress, 1992), p. 244.

[9]Paul Hinnebusch, ed., *Contemplation and Charismatic Renewal* (New York: Paulist, 1986).

[10]M. Basil Pennington, *Centering Prayer: Renewing an Ancient Christian Prayer Form* (New York: Doubleday, 1980), p. 169, and Thomas Keating, *Open Mind, Open Heart: The Contemplative Dimension of the Gospel* (Rockport, Mass: Element, 1986), pp. 79-80.

[11]Garry Friesen, *Decision Making and the Will of God: A Biblical Alternative to the Traditional View* (Portland, Ore.: Multnomah Press, 1980).

Chapter 14: Healing: Transforming Love

[1]Kenneth F. W. Prior, *The Way of Holiness* (Chicago: Inter-Varsity Press, 1967); Peter Toon, *Justification and Sanctification* (Westchester, Ill.: Crossway Books, 1983); and Melvin Dieter et al., *Five Views on Sanctification* (Grand Rapids, Mich.: Zondervan, 1987).

[2]J. I. Packer, *Rediscovering Holiness* (Ann Arbor, Mich.: Servant Books, 1992).

[3]Richard J. Foster, *Celebration of Discipline: The Path to Spiritual Growth* (New York: Harper & Row, 1978).

[4]On the spirituality of social justice, see Richard J. Foster and James B. Smith, eds., *Devotional Classics: Selected Readings for Individuals and Groups* (San Francisco: HarperSanFrancisco, 1993), pp. 145-201.

[5]Hendrikus Berkhof, *Christian Faith: An Introduction to the Study of the Faith* (Grand Rapids, Mich.: Eerdmans, 1979), pp. 499-520.

[6]Morton T. Kelsey, *Healing and Christianity in Ancient Thought and Modern Times* (New York: Harper & Row, 1973).

[7]Francis MacNutt, *Healing* (Notre Dame, Ind.: Ave Maria, 1974).

[8]John Wimber and Kevin Springer, *Power Healing* (San Francisco: Harper & Row, 1987), and Charles H. Kraft, *Christianity with Power: Your Worldview and Your Experience of the Supernatural* (Ann Arbor, Mich.: Servant, 1989).

[9]Jon Ruthven, *On the Cessation of the Charismata: The Protestant Polemic on Postbiblical Miracles* (Sheffield, U.K.: Sheffield Academic Press, 1993).

[10]Kraft, *Christianity with Power.*

Chapter 15: Bible: Feeding Love

[1]Wilfred C. Smith, *What Is Scripture? A Comparative Approach* (Minneapolis: Fortress, 1993).

[2]On inspiration, see Paul J. Achtemeier, *The Inspiration of Scripture: Problems and Proposals* (Philadelphia: Westminster Press, 1980), Bruce Vawter, *Biblical Inspiration* (London: Hutchinson, 1972), and William J. Abraham, *The Divine Inspiration of Holy Scripture* (New York: Oxford University Press, 1981).

[3]James D. G. Dunn, "The Authority of the Scripture According to Scripture," in *The Living Word* (London: SCM Press, 1987), pp. 89-136.

[4]Hans Küng, *Christianity and the World Religions* (New York: Doubleday, 1986), pp. 19-36.

[5]Jean Levie, *The Bible: Word of God in Words of Men* (London: Chapman, 1961), and Clark H. Pinnock, *The Scripture Principle* (San Francisco: Harper & Row, 1984), pt. 2.

[6]Stanley J. Grenz, *Revisioning Evangelical Theology: A Fresh Agenda for the Twenty-first Century* (Downers Grove, Ill.: InterVarsity Press, 1993), chap. 5.

[7]Donald K. McKim, *What Christians Believe About the Bible* (Nashville: Thomas Nelson, 1985), and David H. Kelsey, *The Uses of Scripture in Recent Theology* (Philadelphia: Fortress, 1975).

[8]Ben F. Meyer, "The Primacy of the Intended Sense of Texts," in *Critical Realism and the New Testament* (Allison Park, Penn.: Pickwick, 1989), pp. 17-55.

[9]Grant R. Osborne, *The Hermeneutical Spiral: A Comprehensive Introduction to Biblical Interpretation* (Downers Grove, Ill.: InterVarsity Press, 1991), and Anthony C. Thiselton, *New Horizons in Hermeneutics* (Grand Rapids, Mich.: Zondervan, 1992). Osborne deals more with the horizon of the text and Thiselton more with the horizon of the reader.

[10]Sandra M. Schneiders, *The Revelatory Text: Interpreting the New Testament as Sacred Scripture* (San Francisco: HarperSanFrancisco, 1991).

[11]Jeanne Guyon, *Experiencing the Depths of Jesus* (Goleta, Calif.: Christian Books, 1975).

[12]Craig S. Keener, *Paul, Women and Wives: Marriage and Women's Ministry in the Letters*

of Paul (Peabody, Mass.: Hendrickson, 1992), p. 35.
[13]Willard M. Swartley, *Slavery, Sabbath, War and Women: Case Issues in Biblical Interpretation* (Scottdale, Penn.: Herald Press, 1983).

Chapter 16: Fellowship: Enjoying Love
[1]Jürgen Moltmann, *The Church in the Power of the Spirit: A Contribution to Messianic Ecclesiology* (London: SCM Press, 1977), pp. 314-17.
[2]Jürgen Moltmann, *The Trinity and the Kingdom* (San Francisco: Harper & Row, 1981), pp. 212-22.
[3]Alan J. Roxburgh, *Reaching a New Generation: Strategies for Tomorrow's Church* (Downers Grove, Ill.: InterVarsity Press, 1993), chap. 7.
[4]This is a major theme in Stanley J. Grenz, *Theology for the Community of God* (Nashvile: Broadman & Holman, 1994).
[5]On the bodily gestures of love, see Jürgen Moltmann, *The Spirit of Life: A Univeral Affirmation* (Minneapolis: Fortress, 1992), pp. 263-67.
[6]Howard A. Snyder, *Signs of the Spirit: How God Reshapes the Church* (Grand Rapids, Mich.: Zondervan, 1989).
[7]David L. Watson, *The Early Methodist Class Meeting* (Nashville: Discipleship Resources, 1985), and *Covenant Discipleship: Christian Formation Through Mutual Accountability* (Nashville: Discipleship Resources, 1991).
[8]Howard A. Snyder, *The Problem of Wineskins* (Downers Grove, Ill.: InterVarsity Press, 1975), chap. 11.
[9]Richard Mouw, "Humility, Hope and the Divine Slowness," in *How My Mind Has Changed*, ed. James M. Wall and David Heim (Grand Rapids, Mich.: Ecrdmans, 1991), pp. 21-31.

Conclusion
[1]Karl Barth, *Church Dogmatics* 2/1 (Edinburgh: T & T Clark, 1957), p. 656.
[2]Henri Boulad, *All Is Grace: God and the Mystery of Time* (New York: Crossroad, 1991).